Literature Circles
Cooperative Learning for Grades 3-8

Mimi Neamen
and
Mary Strong

Illustrated by Karen Servatt

1992
TEACHER IDEAS PRESS
A Division of
Libraries Unlimited, Inc.
Englewood, Colorado

TEACHER IDEAS PRESS
A Division of
Libraries Unlimited, Inc.
P.O. Box 6633
Englewood, Colorado 80155-6633

Library of Congress Cataloging-in-Publication Data
Neamen, Mimi.
    Literature circles : cooperative learning for grades 3-8 / Mimi
Neamen and Mary Strong ; illustrated by Karen Servatt.
    xiv, 103 p., 22x28 cm.
    Includes bibliographical references and index.
    ISBN 0-87287-987-9 (soft)
    1. Literature--Study and teaching (Elementary)--United States.
2. Group work in education. 3. Children--Books and reading.
I. Strong, Mary, 1940-   . II. Title.
LB1575.5.U5N43 1992   92-3681
                                                 CIP

Contents

Acknowledgments

We thank our husbands and our children for their patience and support as we worked on this book. (They've become excellent cooks in the process.)

The Teacher Enhancement Program, a collaborative program between the University of New Mexico and the Albuquerque Public Schools, and Dr. Richard Van Dongen provided the assistance and opportunities needed so work on this book could proceed.

Glenda Armstrong, the school librarian, accommodated us in every way imaginable.

Karen Servatt, the illustrator, captured her insight into each book in vivid pen-and-ink images.

Administrators encouraged us to cross school boundaries and gave us freedom to develop new ideas.

Colleagues took our projects into their classrooms and made them their own.

Some students came to our classes willingly and eagerly and some came because there was nowhere else to go after the buses dropped them off. They constantly renewed our faith in kids' ability to learn and grow.

We believe in the inquisitiveness of young minds. We wrote this book for them; they are responsible for the direction it has taken.

Introduction

The Master is at work in the garden. With pruning shears in hand, the Master bends over each new, growing plant. The Master prunes off a tip here or a wayward tendril there, urging the plant to follow its most graceful inclination. Sometimes pruning restores health to a plant or removes dead wood. Always pruning enhances helping the plant follow its most natural and eloquent bent. Finding curves more appealing than straight lines, the Master encourages each plant to stretch harmoniously, occasionally tying down a limb so the wind doesn't break it off. Waiting for flowers to appear before doing any pruning, choosing the strongest canes to remain and removing weak canes that sap strength, protecting new and fragile buds, and pruning at a particular spot so that growth takes a certain path are all facets of the technique of the Master gardener.

In teaching, there are also those who know their craft. The Master in the classroom works with children, enhancing their own ways and directions, finding strengths, accentuating curves rather than linear growth, acknowledging gracefulness and beauty, encouraging growth in a particular direction, and waiting patiently for the blossoming that comes in its own season.

The Master gardener trusts nature: sod, nutrients, sunlight, and rain. The Master uses pruning shears carefully to nip and guide each individual branch. The Master has no use for an electric hedge trimmer that shears everything at the same level. The Master coaxes tender limbs onto a trellis that illuminates the plant's beauty, rather than nailing the stalk onto a post. The Master nurtures each plant's natural inclination and champions its imaginative agility.

The Master teacher trusts that students are hearing, absorbing, and learning in their own way and their own time. The Master knows that connections are being made and will continue to be made. The Master believes the learning opportunities in writing and reading will build by small increments into knowledge.

The Master—trusting, nurturing, believing, and knowing—watches the garden bloom and flourish.

Literature Circles: Cooperative Learning for Grades 3-8 is for public and private school teachers of intermediate-grade students. Although much of the material in the book is written for teachers, there are many reproducible pages for students. The material can be adapted to any teaching style, but it may also be used in the format given.

In this book, a *literature circle* is a group of students reading the same novel, and *cooperative learning* refers to a group working together on the novel to accomplish a common goal or product.

In the book we refer to B- and C-level special education students. B-level students receive one hour of special help per day. C-level students receive two or more hours of special help per day.

Our purpose is to address the nationwide educational trend toward literature-based reading programs, student choice, cooperative learning, heterogeneous grouping, and performance-based assessment. The program benefits not only the group but also each individual student; it increases the amount of reading students do, provides opportunities for inquiry and critical thinking, and teaches students how to work cooperatively.

Our program is based on beliefs, assumptions, and observations of how kids learn. Our concept of reading and its counterpart, writing, and their processes led us to create a structure within which all students can be successful readers. This program combines literature circles and cooperative learning in a way that provides opportunities for decision making, which in turn builds a natural relationship between content and process.

Submerging students in a young adult novel using this format creates a community of learners who are finding a way to reach a common goal. The natural engagement in dialogue about their reading nurtures affective and social learning as well as helps them grasp specific knowledge. The cooperative learning is a support system upon which students build their understanding of a particular novel. In the literature circles, all group members meet on an equal basis, regardless of reading ability, to contribute to a final project that is realized through the combined strengths of all members. The evaluation system ensures that each student is graded not only on group participation and meeting deadlines but also on the quality and appropriateness of his or her contributions.

Literature Circles is divided into three chapters. Chapter 1 explains the novel projects, tells how to use them, and explains the student reproducible pages. Chapter 2 contains short projects using picture books. These projects are especially helpful in readying students to work cooperatively with longer works. Chapter 3 contains cooperative learning projects for 28 novels. The novels are arranged according to reading level, beginning with the easier books.

Teachers may use one novel at a time in the classroom, breaking into cooperative learning groups to complete the projects; or they may use several of the novels simultaneously, forming cooperative learning groups according to the students' reading choices. The complexity and depth of the involvement in the projects will vary according to the age and intellectual maturity of the students.

While all instructional and evaluative material is included in the first chapter, activities for each novel project are grouped as follows: short summary of the novel, vocabulary list, and novel projects.

The literature circles may be interspersed with other activities throughout the year, or they may be used as the entire literature focus of the year. We hope that *Literature Circles: Cooperative Learning for Grades 3-8* will be useful to all teachers who believe both in the magic and the educational value of reading and in the "joy of story."

1   HOW TO TEACH WITH LITERATURE CIRCLES

HOW TO USE THE NOVEL PROJECTS

The following projects use cooperative learning as a base for working with and learning about a novel. The cooperative aspect is stressed in all projects as the students work together to complete assignments using their chosen novel.

The following are merely suggestions, not dictums. We share the strategies and procedures that have worked well for us. Feel free to make changes according to your classroom population. Throughout this section, we give reasons for doing things in certain ways. We also cite examples of how certain students performed in various situations. In every way we seek to communicate to the students that we value time spent reading, that ownership of the work to come lies with the students, that opportunities will be provided for group decision making and goal setting, that we trust their ability to make good decisions, and that there is a reason to read the novel.

The flexible nature of this book accommodates a wide range of learning styles, and each novel project contains activities that address social skill objectives, affective objectives, and knowledge objectives. Although we had preconceived notions of what the outcomes of each project would be as we designed them, experience has taught us that many interpretations are possible. Because two broad objectives of cooperative learning in literature circles are to promote problem finding as well as problem solving and to create questions as well as answers, this phenomenon of varying interpretations is one of the beauties of the learning that occurs.

Finally, although we do use and will continue to use these projects in contained classrooms, we feel that cross-grade-level use of the material is most beneficial to students. The older students set a good example for the younger ones; they demonstrate how responsible they are due to their older age. The younger students emulate the learning behaviors of the older students.

Choosing a Novel

Choice is essential in creating an environment in which students want to learn. We suggest that groups be formed not by arbitrary or heterogeneous groupings formulated by the teacher but by student choice. We believe choice allows students to exert ownership, and ownership ensures that students will take the best path for their own learning. The reading level of a book is not a main consideration when forming groups; students will readily read a novel if *they* have chosen it. The novels in this book are arranged from lowest to highest reading levels as a convenience to readers.

The following method of selection is suggested because it gives each student a choice.

1. The teacher selects the novels from which the students may choose. There should be five copies of each book because five is the optimum number for a cooperative learning group.

2. The teacher gives a short "book talk" on each title so the students have a basis for selection.

   > ■ Heads are turned toward the teacher as she holds up each book and offers a glimpse into the story between its covers. Adam's attention is riveted on the book *Where the Red Fern Grows*. He listens intently to the book talk because he knows he will soon be asked to choose one of the books being introduced. Nick makes a few notes about each novel, and Michael smiles and nods his head as he recognizes a familiar author.

3. Students draw numbers to be used in the selection process.

4. The teacher lists each novel on the board with five slots for students' names under each novel. Be sure to have at least five more total slots than you have students; this assures that the student who has drawn the last number also has a choice.

5. The student who draws number 1 begins the selection process. As students choose, their names are written under the appropriate novel title. When a particular novel group is filled, students must choose from the other available titles. Complete the selection process with all students.

For a class of 25 students, you might choose the following novels and set up your chalkboard in the following manner:

Red Fern

1._____
2._____
3._____
4._____
5._____

Gilly Hopkins

1._____
2._____
3._____
4._____
5._____

Trouble River

1._____
2._____
3._____
4._____
5._____

Blue Dolphins

1._____
2._____
3._____
4._____
5._____

Sing ... Moon

1._____
2._____
3._____
4._____
5._____

Black Star

1._____
2._____
3._____
4._____
5._____

The total of 30 slots allows for 5 more slots than there are students. This is very important, because the student who draws number 25 needs to have a choice of novels. Some groups will not be comprised of the optimum number of five members, but they will still work well.

If you have chosen to integrate two classrooms when working with the projects, each class should draw numbers separately. The fifth grader who draws number 1 should choose first and then the sixth grader who draws number 1. The number of novels from which to choose must increase accordingly. Also, try to mix the classes. For instance, if *Where the Red Fern Grows* is filling up with sixth graders (three have already chosen this book), tell the sixth graders that this particular novel is no longer a choice for them.

■ For the most part, students choose books that interest them, rather than choosing to be with their friends. Tina, who drew number 3, chooses *The Great Gilly Hopkins*. Her best friend, Angela, who drew number 7, sees that there is still room in that group. She hesitates as Tina points toward the chalkboard and then places her hands in a prayer position and mouths "Please." Angela is in a quandary. Should she be in the group with Tina, or should she read the book that really interests her? "*Trouble River*," Angela says when her number is called. "Tina, I really wanna see how the grandma floats down the river in her rocking chair. You remember that great rocking chair my grandma has...."

Beginning the Group Work

1. Ask students to sit with their groups.

2. Pass out the novels.

3. Give each group the novel folder (to be kept at all times in the classroom). The folder contains the following items:
   • Group worksheet (one copy; see page 12)
   • Individual Book Checklist (five copies; see page 9)
   • Group Novel Checklist (one copy; see page 10)
   • Daily checklist (one copy, preferably stapled to one side of the folder; see page 11)
   • Group Projects (five copies)

4. Appoint a facilitator and a checker for each group for the first day.

5. Have each student fill out the Individual Book Checklist.

6. Have each group determine how many pages (or chapters) should be read each day to complete the book in the time allotted (determined by the teacher). (We have found that 10 school days is ample time. This is shown later in the sample timeline in figure 1.1 on page 7.)

> ■ The group reading *The Great Gilly Hopkins* was counting out the pages attempting to find a way to "chunk" the reading. Heather was counting, "18, 19, 20..." when Stephen glanced over at the group that had chosen *Where the Red Fern Grows*. They had already finished dividing the book into ten "chunks."
> "How didja do that?" Stephen asked.
> "We divided the total number of pages in the book by ten."
> Meanwhile, the group reading *Trouble River* had divided the total number of chapters in the book by ten to determine how much they would have to read each day.

7. The checker fills out the Group Novel Checklist and the Daily Checklist.

8. The facilitator reads aloud the Group Worksheet. This explains the functions of the group and the duties of both the facilitator and the checker. These duties will rotate daily, thus ensuring that each student plays a leadership role in the group.

9. The facilitator reads aloud the Group Projects while students follow on their own copies. Any questions concerning projects should be discussed at this time.

10. The group decides whether class time will be spent reading, working on projects, or doing a combination of both. The reading can be accomplished in any way the students choose.

> ■ The groups had spaced themselves around the room. One quiet, calm group was in the center, a vision of relaxed absorption in contrast to the bustle of activity surrounding it. This group had elected to read during class on this day. Adam's legs were over the back of his chair, his fingers pursing his lower lip, and his book was in his lap. Juanita, Jon, and Nick had also snuggled into comfortable positions. The teacher noticed and watched this group with wonderment. Two of the four students, Adam and Nick, were mainstreamed B-level special education students. Each had experienced attention-deficit problems, yet *Where the Red Fern Grows* had them completely mesmerized.

Working with Group Projects

Vocabulary: You may choose whether or not to use the vocabulary lists given at the beginning of each novel project. If you use them, ask students to discuss the words as they find them in the text. They should try to determine the meaning in context, and the dictionary should only be used as a last resort. Another way to work with vocabulary is to have students generate their own lists. We have found that completing the vocabulary work is the least enjoyable and satisfactory project for our students; therefore, in our classrooms, we do not use the vocabulary. We have, however, included the work for teachers who feel their students need it.

Group Projects: The projects are self-explanatory. Students may complete the projects in the manner that best suits their group. Some groups do all the projects together. They work on them in class, and they get together after school and on weekends to complete the tasks. Some groups choose to divide the work among the members. We believe students will make the best choice possible for themselves and their group. It is important that students be able to make these choices and take responsibility for them.

We always give students an option of creating a project of their own that they feel will demonstrate their knowledge of the novel. If they want to do something different that is worthwhile, we enable them either to substitute it for one of the given projects or to do it as an extra project. Many of our students have done work that we never would have dreamed of assigning. For example, one group who read *My Side of the Mountain* fixed an entire meal for a group of 50 students. They served venison stew, fruit soup, baked turnips (roots), and corn bread (acorn bread). The class enjoyed the 9:00 A.M. meal. Another group who read *Snow Treasure* wanted to write a rap about the book. We couldn't imagine a rap on this topic, and the students surprised us with a rhythmical and knowledgeable representation of the book. Other groups may choose a "resident artist," a "resident builder," or a "resident writer." Students are chosen for these jobs because they have particular talents in that area. One of our C-level students is not at his best when reading and writing, but his superb artistic talent was recognized, and he was chosen as resident artist for his group. Usually, this student does not experience much success in school, but in the literature circles he attained scholastic victory. The group applauded his talent, and they gave him an "A" in the subsequent evaluation. Many students who do not usually shine in their academic life find that they can be a "star" in literature circles because their talents are appreciated.

> ■ Santos has trouble with written language. Unable to spell correctly, he hesitates to contribute to written projects. He is, however, recognized by his peers for his artistic abilities and clever ideas. He became his group's "artist in residence" after guiding them back and forth, into and through the text of *Island of the Blue Dolphins* in order to accurately create a clay model of Karana's island.
>
> "No! That's not the way it should look!" Santos said. "Let me show you where it says it in the book." Santos flipped through the book until he found the passage he wanted and then showed it to the rest of his group.
>
> "Okay, okay. We'll do it that way," Jack said as he began to reshape the clay. "We oughta listen to him the first time," he said under his breath to no one in particular.
>
> When Jack was finished, Santos gave him the "high five" sign and said, "Right on!"

Finding Descriptive Phrases

One project we use with every novel is "finding descriptive phrases." We ask students to find 25 phrases in the novel that they think are especially descriptive and that create vivid pictures in their minds. They copy the phrase (enclosed in quotation marks) and illustrate it. Then they make and present to the group a "Book of Descriptive Phrases." Looking for and finding these phrases makes the students examine the author's style. After students have looked for descriptive phrases, shades of Wilson Rawls, Katherine Paterson, or Scott O'Dell creep into their own writing. Once they have looked for these kinds of passages in several novels by different authors, students begin to meld the various styles and eventually come up with one that suits them. Though we did not include this in every novel packet, we do use it with each book. You, of course, may choose whether or not to use this activity.

> ■ "What are you doing?" James asked, pointing to Billy's illustration of a phrase containing the word faun.
>
> Surprised, Billy answered, "I'm drawing a picture of a baby deer. Can't you see that?"
>
> "A faun isn't a baby deer. It's a man with a goat's body," James explained. "Do you know the difference between faun and fawn?" He pointed as he said, "This one has a 'u,' and this one has a 'w'."
>
> "Neat!" Billy said. "Where didja learn that?"

Using Generic Activities

Many activities and projects can be used with any and every book. These include mobiles, dioramas, simple murals, mini-television-shows, puppet shows, and timelines of the plot. We prefer to use activities specific to each novel, but these somewhat "pedestrian" activities can prove to very useful, especially for beginning literature circle students. They provide a comfortable form in which to present a not so comfortable content. Dealing with form and content together can sometimes be overwhelming for budding cooperative learners. As classroom teacher you know the students best, and you must judge which methods will best accommodate your students.

■ Stephanie was crying again. "Mrs. Strong, Heather doesn't like the box I brought for our TV. She won't let me use it."

"It falls over," pouted Heather as she demonstrated the instability of Stephanie's TV.

"Could you compromise?" suggested Mrs. Strong. Heather, not a good group worker at this point in the year, pouted even more. The teacher got two bookends from the cupboard. "Could you use these to prop it up?"

Stephanie and Heather left to try the bookends. This solution, however, proved to be only a bandage for the problem. The real trouble was discovered a short time later. Heather wanted to use the box TV that she had made. Days later, the girls worked out a compromise themselves; they placed Heather's TV inside of Stephanie's TV. Both TVs were used, and Stephanie's didn't topple.

Presenting the Work

Presentation day (or days) is the culmination of the time spent on the projects. The time allotted for this varies with the intricacies of and time needed for the presentations. Some groups (especially the ones serving food) will need more time than others. It is important, though, not to rush any group; they have worked long and hard, and they need to know that their work is valued.

Gather the entire class and determine the order for the presentations (unless one or more groups specifically ask to be first). We always try to put the "food" groups last, because this allows students to enjoy the goodies and there needs to be time for cleanup. Caution each group to have their projects ready and assembled and tell them that any special equipment needs to be on hand.

A few days before the final presentations, groups need to be reminded to practice the presentations. Until they have done it once (and sometimes not even then), they don't realize how much organization is required for the final presentation.

■ Tracy and Annette looked at the french onion soup. "It looks like onions swimming in a dirty swimming pool. Yuk!" No one would try the soup that was something Sam might have eaten in *My Side of the Mountain*. The class athlete swaggered up to the group who was serving the disgusting-looking brown soup. He asked for some, tasted it, turned to face his classmates, and said, "Good stuff." A line formed in front of the crockpot.

Shy Rachel, as her part in the presentation, demonstrated the folk art project for *Charley Skedaddle*: holes punched in copper sheeting to create a pattern.

Students donned their party hats and retrieved their invitations as they lined up for cake, ice cream, and party favors for *There's a Boy in the Girls' Bathroom*.

There was something for everyone. It was a morning spent enjoying each other's creativity and imagination as students shared the conversations from the works they had read.

Evaluating the Groups

Performance-based assessment is often very difficult. We use a two-part system that we have found to be very successful, and our students and their parents consider it very fair as well as useful concerning students' future performance. Students fill out the following form on page 13 twice during the project—once at the halfway point and once at the end. After students have filled out the forms, they discuss the results with the teacher and the other group members. Each student tells what grade he or she assigned to each of the other group members and, most importantly, why that grade was assigned. Students often perceive their own contributions very differently from how others perceive them. There is always a marked difference in the quality of group interaction and sharing the day after the midpoint evaluation. One student who had done excellent work on the projects could not understand why the group graded him low until they told him that he never conferred—he merely assumed that the rest of the group would like what he was doing. He began talking about the projects with the group, and everyone saw the quality of the projects improve. (See page 13 for reproducible.)

Dealing with Disruptive Group Members

What do you do with a student who is consistently disrupting the group? Of course, students should be informed at the onset that disruptive behavior will not be allowed. If a student persists in this type of behavior, the group may vote to remove him or her from the group, but the group must justify their decision. Any student ejected from a group must complete all of the projects alone. Most students don't want to do all of the work by themselves, so disruptive behavior in a group is usually minimal. We have had, at different times, two students who were kicked out of their groups. They were both upset and begged to be re-admitted, but the groups would not reconsider. One student did all of the work; one did not. They were graded accordingly, and both students were better group members the next time. We feel that the group, not the teacher, has to have this power. A student chooses to be disruptive and uncooperative, and the groups need to be able to choose to dismiss such a student.

■ After two weeks, Stephen demonstrated to his *Pinballs* group that he was uninterested in being a contributing group member. He was, in fact, disruptive. The group members voted with good reason to eject him from the group. Stephen finished the projects by himself, and he was responsible for all the work. He sat in with the group during the final evaluation and heard from his peers how they perceived his performance in the group. When Stephen chose to read *The Sign of the Beaver* later in the year, he was an exemplary group member; he received all "A's" on his final evaluations. Many evaluations stated, "Stephen is always serious about his work and does his share."

Other Considerations

Journal writing. Ten quiet writing minutes in journals at the end of a day's work in literature circles gives students the opportunity to examine what was going on within their groups and to assess their group's operation. Voluntary sharing of the journal entries afterward often opens up conversations that enable the entire class to process the day's activity and provides helpful insights to the teacher.

■ Lukas was eager to share his journal entry. "Today in our Literature Circles, our group did a little bit on the sled, and Tania and Trent went to the library to do some more research on the Iditarod. I am going to do a lot of research on Eskimos and their beliefs tonight at home."

Later, Mike shared his entry privately with the teacher. "My group wants me to give them my work so they can get credit for it, and I can't. I have worked on the wolf behavior and they want to copy it."

That same day Logan wrote, "Mike got all mad because he thinks Allison wants to get all the credit, but all she wants to do is type it over. We started the other projects without Mike. He's still got it all wrong. I hope things go much better tomorrow."

Sure enough, Mike wrote the next day, "Today our group worked a lot better, and we got a lot of work done. We also know what we have to do. We did not argue today at all ... I liked today a lot. We have lots to do, but if we work like we have today, we'll get it all done."

Special education students. We arrange schedules so our special education students are always included in literature circles. We have found that the nature of the novel projects and the group work allows and even encourages these students to blossom. Also, we know of several self-contained special education classrooms that are successfully incorporating this work in their curriculum.

No labels are attached to these students, especially when grade levels are mixed. Their book choice is not restricted, and we have found that their reading and participation are on a par with that of their peers. These projects afford the opportunity for equal status among group members, a primary consideration for special education students. The implications for the success of special education students participating in cooperative learning in literature circles are limitless.

Malfunctioning groups. Don't focus on groups that seem to be malfunctioning. Instead, focus on and praise loudly (within earshot of the malfunctioning group) the groups that are working well. Be specific in your praise so the "target" group will know exactly how to improve their performance. It is very difficult not to talk directly to a malfunctioning group about their difficulties, but the results are much better if the group thinks they have solved their problems by themselves. The sharing of journal entries is often very helpful for such groups.

Reading aloud. At the beginning of each session, we read a picture book aloud. This serves two main purposes. First, it calms and quiets the students and gives them all a common point of reference for the day. Second, it focuses their attention on language—a primary concern in literature circles.

Using the library. Each book project involves some kind of research. We feel students learn to use and know the library not through skill drills but through information gathering that is pertinent to them. We want them to have a plan in mind, however, when they visit the library, and for this reason we use two guides. (See pages 14 and 15 for student reproducibles.)

Total time:	3 weeks and 4 days (2 weeks to complete reading, 1 week to finish projects, 2 days for presentation, 2 days for evaluation)
Day 1	1. Students draw numbers. 2. Teacher gives book talks. 3. Students choose books. 4. Books are passed out. 5. Deadline for completion of reading is set and calendar of events is discussed.
Day 2	1. Group procedures and activities are discussed. 2. Groups divide reading into "chunks." 3. Checklists are filled out. 4. Students begin reading.
Days 3-11	Students read books and work as group members on the activities and at the group's own speed, keeping in mind the date by which all work must be finished.
Day 9	Midterm evaluations are completed and discussed.
Day 11	Reading is completed.
Days 12-16	Students work on group projects and activities and prepare for presentations.
Days 17 & 18	Group presentations are made to entire class.
Days 19 & 20	Final evaluations are filled out and discussed with group and teacher.

Fig. 1.1. Sample Timeline for a Three-Week Cooperative Literature Circle Project.

HOW TO USE STUDENT REPRODUCIBLE PAGES

The following items should be kept in each group's folder.

Individual Book Checklist (five copies, or enough for each group member): The purpose of this sheet is twofold: The teacher has a list of each student's book and book number, and the student knows by looking at the sheet how many pages must be read each day. Each student should fill out this sheet with name, book title, book number, and the number of pages to be read each day. The group's first cooperative task is to decide how to divide the reading.

Group Novel Checklist (one copy): This master list of group members and their book numbers is completed by the checker.

Daily Checklist (one copy, preferably stapled to the folder): This evaluation of each group member's daily performance is completed at the end of the day by the checker. The evaluation criteria are listed on the sheet. This sheet is a means by which students can see how they need to improve their work in the group. The teacher can also see, at a quick glance, how the various group members perceive each other's contribution to the project. This is a very valuable aid to the final evaluation process.

Group Worksheet (one copy): This sheet is read aloud to the group by the facilitator to explain how the group functions and to define the roles of both checker and facilitator. Members of the group may want to refer to this sheet from time to time to clarify roles or responsibilities.

The following items are reproducibles and are not included in group folders.

Group Evaluation Form: One copy of this reproducible is given to each student at both the mid-project evaluation and the final evaluation. Each student is asked to honestly and conscientiously fill out the evaluation form. Tell students not to merely rely on their memories but also to look at the Daily Checklist for specific information. It is very important that students give reasons for their grades. After Group Evaluation Forms have been completed, meet with each group and discuss the grades with the group. A consensus should be reached and a grade assigned in each group.

Before Going to the Library and *Finding Descriptors along the Way* (see pages 14 and 15): These two reproducibles concerning the library are designed to help students make good use of their library time. You must decide how and when to use these guides. Some teachers place five copies of each in the group project folders; others pass the sheets out to students as they journey to the library.

(Text continues page 16.)

INDIVIDUAL BOOK CHECKLIST

Name:_____

Title of Book:_____

Book Number: _____

Number of Pages to Be Read Each Day:_____

From *Literature Circles*, 1992. Teacher Ideas Press • P.O. Box 6633 • Englewood, CO 80155-6633.

GROUP NOVEL CHECKLIST

Title of Book:_____

Names of Group Members:

1._____

Book #_____

2._____

Book #_____

3._____

Book #_____

4._____

Book #_____

5._____

Book #_____

From *Literature Circles*, 1992. Teacher Ideas Press • P.O. Box 6633 • Englewood, CO 80155-6633.

DAILY CHECKLIST

Book Title:_____

Date

Name

1._____

2._____

3._____

4._____

5._____

Checker's Initials

Instructions for grading

1. If the group member has read the assigned number of pages or chapters for the previous day, place a plus (+) in the upper right-hand corner of the appropriate box. If the group member has not completed the assigned reading, place a minus (—) in the upper right-hand corner of the appropriate box. Do this at the beginning of each work session.

2. Grade daily group participation in the following manner:
   3 = Good participation
   2 = Medium participation
   1 = Little participation
   0 = No participation

   Place the assigned number in the appropriate box at the end of the group work session.

GROUP WORKSHEET

You will read your book individually. How you choose to read is up to you. You may choose to do all reading at home, either silently or with a parent or sibling. You may choose to read in class, either silently or aloud. You also may choose to do a combination of both.

All the work on the group projects will be done together. When discussing how the projects will be completed, you should follow three rules of good group discussion:

1.   Give everyone a fair turn.

2.   Give reasons for ideas.

3.   Give different ideas.

Each group will have a facilitator and a checker to ensure that the criteria for good group discussion are met. The roles of facilitator and checker will rotate on a daily basis. Each group member will probably fulfill each role at least three times during the span of the project.

Facilitator: The facilitator sees to it that everyone in the group has an equal amount of time to talk and to listen. The facilitator is also responsible for seeking answers to questions within the group. If the group is unable to answer a question, only the facilitator is permitted to ask the teacher or the librarian for help.

Checker: The checker fills in the Daily Checklist appropriately each day.

GROUP EVALUATION FORM

In the space provided below, list each member of your group. Evaluate each person according to the following criteria (use the Daily Checklists to help you in your evaluation):

1. Equal share of work (or extra)

2. Consistently a good group member

3. Dependable

4. Reading always completed on time

5. Contributed ideas to the group

6. Work done neatly and with pride

Give each person a grade (A, B, C, D, or F) and tell *why* you think the person deserves that grade. Be honest.

1. Name_____ Grade_____

2. Name_____ Grade_____

3. Name_____ Grade_____

4. Name_____ Grade_____

5. Your Name_____ Grade_____

From *Literature Circles*, 1992. Teacher Ideas Press • P.O. Box 6633 • Englewood, CO 80155-6633.

BEFORE GOING TO THE LIBRARY

"Brainstorm" in your group before you go to the library. Ask yourselves questions about what you need to find and where you can look for it.

Examples: Need a map?

Questions—What part of the country? the world?

Is it a real town?

What library tools have maps? (atlases and encyclopedias)

Want pictures of Alaska? Look in magazines, encyclopedias, and nonfiction books about Alaska.

Are you looking for a person or people? Check an encyclopedia index, a bibliographical dictionary, biography, or a magazine index.

Are you looking for a place? Check an atlas, an encyclopedia, a geographical dictionary, or a magazine index.

Are you looking for a thing or an event? Check an encyclopedia index or the card catalog for non-fiction books.

FINDING DESCRIPTORS ALONG THE WAY

As you read about your topic, keep a list of descriptors that relate to your focus.

1. Terms and key words

2. People

3. Places

4. Events

From *Literature Circles*, 1992. Teacher Ideas Press • P.O. Box 6633 • Englewood, CO 80155-6633.

2 LITERATURE CIRCLES WITH PICTURE BOOKS

USING PICTURE BOOKS BEFORE YOU BEGIN

Often students are not familiar with cooperative learning, especially as it is associated with literature. You can introduce your class to the concept on a somewhat smaller scale with the following miniprojects using picture books. Like the novel projects, these may be used in the manner you choose. We have found that classes readily adapt to the cooperative learning format when going from the simpler picture-book projects to the more complex novel projects.

We recommend the suggested forms and techniques even for the shorter books. This way students become acquainted with the procedure before they go on to the novel projects. We include several picture books to provide various options.

1. Arbitrarily divide the class into groups. Read aloud a picture book and discuss the projects for that book as an entire class. Then have each group complete the same project in the same way at the same time. This emphasizes cooperative learning: how each student functions for the benefit of the whole group. (Many teachers have found this method very helpful because they don't have as many "group" problems once the students fully understand their roles in a cooperative learning situation.)

2. Arbitrarily divide the class into groups. Read aloud a picture book. Then have each group complete the projects for that book. (You will notice that each group's interpretation of a project will differ. This gives the students a good idea of the possibilities offered by this method of study.)

3. Choose five or six picture books and give a short book talk about each one. Complete the selection process (a good way for students to learn how the novels are selected), and begin group work.

We believe in the use of picture books in any classroom. We love the stories, the illustrations, and the way of presenting information. Picture books are also used in many novel projects because we feel they enhance the projects.

LON PO PO
Ed Young
Philomel Books, 1989

Examining Gingko Nuts

Is the gingko nut "real" or "imaginary"? Go to the library and find out about gingko nuts. Whether the nuts are real or imaginary, you can complete the following project. The gingko nut grows on a tree. What does that tree look like? What kind of leaves does it have? What does the nut itself look like? Show your answers to these questions in any format you choose. A paneled mural in the style of Ed Young, using his technique of watercolor and pastels, is one option; a three-dimensional tree is another. Use your own imagination to accomplish this project.

Telling a Red Riding Hood Story

There are many versions of the Red Riding Hood tale. Either find another one in the library or write one of your own. If you choose to write your own, be sure to include the following characters: Red Riding Hood, the mother, the grandmother, and the wolf. You may want to try writing the story from another point of view such as the wolf's. The method of presentation is up to the group. Some suggestions are a play, a puppet show, a picture book that you read to the class, an audiocassette complete with background music and sound effects, or a videotape.

Creating a Pictorial "Trickline"

As you read *Lon Po Po*, you will discover the real identity of the wolf through several clues from the author. Make a list of these clues. You will also discover as you read how the children trick the wolf. Make a list of these tricks. Create a "trickline" (like a timeline) that shows pictorially how the identity of the wolf is discovered and how the children trick the wolf. You may want to use different colors—one for discovery and another for tricks. Choose a method that best suits your group.

THE TRUE STORY OF THE THREE LITTLE PIGS!
Jon Scieszka
Viking, 1989

Comparing Tales

This tale, the wolf's version of the story, is quite different from the familiar tale of the three little pigs and the wolf. Often authors create their own accounts of well-known tales (Scieszka did this), and often different versions are found in various parts of the country. The Appalachian version of the classic tale is the following:

Hooks, William H. *The Three Little Pigs and the Fox.* New York: Macmillan, 1989.

Using the classic version, the Scieszka version, and one other (perhaps the Appalachian version by Hooks), make a chart that compares the three. You might want to begin by listing events in the plot, characters, and confrontational situations on three separate pieces of paper. Determine a visually pleasing and informational way of presenting the three diverse tales. Show how they are alike and how they are different. You may want to use pictures, words, or a combination of both. Color-coding the three tales might be helpful for your audience.

Writing Newspaper Articles

Choose another classic tale, such as *Goldilocks and the Three Bears*. Each group member should write a newspaper article in the first person describing one character's viewpoint of the situation. For instance, if the group decides to write about *Hansel and Gretel*, the following five characters might be chosen: Hansel, Gretel, the stepmother, the father, and the witch. Put the stories into a newspaper format. The newspaper should have "photographs," bylines, and a title.

Building the Houses

The construction of the three houses belonging to the pigs was quite different. One was made of straw, one of sticks, and one of bricks. Build replicas of these three houses on one platform. Be sure to include the surrounding landscape.

FLOSSIE & THE FOX
Patricia C. McKissack
Dial Books, 1986

MIRANDY AND BROTHER WIND
Patricia C. McKissack
Alfred A. Knopf, 1988

Comparing Two Books by the Same Author

Flossie & the Fox is a folktale of the rural South. *Mirandy and Brother Wind* is a story based on a true incident that happened to the author's grandparents. Draw a "story map" of the two main characters, Flossie and Mirandy. The maps should be basically pictorial, but they may contain "clue" words to explain the drawings. Each map should have a beginning point (the onset of the story), go through a journey (the plot line of the story), and have an end (the final destination). As you work on this project, think about how you would map an actual trip you were taking, because the "story map" is a trip through the text. Think of each problem or solution to a problem as a town along the way. When you have finished both maps, look at them carefully. Are there any similarities? Can you draw any conclusions concerning the author's style of writing from comparing your maps? Be prepared to show your maps to the entire class, answering the above questions as you explain the journeys of both Flossie and Mirandy.

Illustrating a Story

Just as authors write differently, illustrators also have different ways of illustrating a book. For example, Jerry Pinkney uses people he knows as models for the characters in his books: Mirandy is based on a little girl who lives down the street from him, Brother Wind is based on Pinkney himself, and Grandmama Beasley is modeled after Pinkney's grandmother. Rachel Isadora, in *Flossie & the Fox*, drew on her imagination to create the representations of Flossie and Big Mama. Choose a tale that has roots either in your part of the country or in your own family history. Write and illustrate that tale. Upon what do you base your illustrations? Do you use models, or do you rely on your imagination? Be prepared to share your story, in standard picture-book form (covers, endpapers, title page complete with publishing information, and dedication), with the entire class on presentation day.

Recognizing Dialect

Both of these books incorporate the rich Afro-American dialect of the rural South. Find a few examples of this dialect in each book. Rewrite passages of dialect in the manner in which you would normally speak. Read both the original and the rewritten passages to the class. Afterward, poll the class to find out what style they prefer.

THE MITTEN
Jan Brett
G. P. Putnam's Sons, 1989

Retelling and Illustrating a Familiar Story

The story of the lost mitten is a Ukrainian tale that Jan Brett has adapted and illustrated. Choose a story that all of the group members know, such as a story you heard as children or one that has been popularized by Disney or another moviemaker. Retell and illustrate your chosen tale in the style Brett used in *The Mitten*. Pay particular attention to the borders and the shadowing that occurs inside the mitten on both the left and right borders. Present your picture book to the class on presentation day. Be sure to format your book correctly: covers, endpapers, title page, and dedication.

Investigating Ukraine

Where is Ukraine? An atlas in the library will help you find this area. Using an encyclopedia or some other type of reference book, find out about this region—its geography, climate, people, clothing, and economics. List facts about these topics as you find them. Contact the chamber of commerce or some other source in your own community to get facts about the same topics. Make a chart that compares these characteristics of Ukraine and your community. The chart should be easy to read and understand. Experiment with different chart forms to decide which you want to use.

Creating a Different Ending

Baba did not want to knit white mittens for Nicki because they could be easily lost in the snow. Imagine that Nicki did lose one of the mittens in the snow. When he returns home, what will Baba say? How will Nicki try to excuse his loss of the mitten? Create a dialogue between Baba and Nicki, and choose the method of presentation that best suits your new ending. Some options are written dialogue, presentation by actors either live or on tape, readers' theater, pantomime that "shows" rather than "tells" the story, or a "choose your own adventure" type of ending. Be sure the entire class is familiar with the story and its original ending before you present your new ending.

TWO BAD ANTS
Chris Van Allsburg
Houghton Mifflin, 1988

Investigating Ants

Ants and the habitat they create are quite interesting. Go to the library and research ants, their society, and their dwellings. Either construct an ant farm that shows how the ants build their living space or, using the information you have found, draw a diagram that shows the inside of an "ant hill." Be prepared to explain your project to the class.

Writing a Sequel

A sequel is something that follows or a continuation. Write either a story that follows *Two Bad Ants* (perhaps the ants find something exciting in another room of the house) or a continuation of the same story (maybe the two ants decide to set up a "crystal" business or the queen gets greedy and goes to the kitchen herself). Follow the writing and illustrating techniques of Chris Van Allsburg. Your presentation should be in the form of a picture book. Don't forget to include all the elements of a book: covers, endpapers, title page complete with publishing information, and dedication page. In your presentation, read Van Allsburg's story before sharing your sequel.

Describing Common Things in an Uncommon Way

Van Allsburg describes very familiar items (a lawn, the brick wall of a house, a sugar bowl, a coffee cup, a person's mouth, a toaster, a kitchen faucet, a garbage disposal, a light socket) through the eyes of creatures that are unfamiliar with these objects. Imagine that you are a creature from the animal kingdom. "See" for the first time an object with which a human would be well acquainted, and describe that object through the eyes of your chosen animal. Each member of the group should choose a different creature and a different object. On presentation day read your descriptions aloud and ask the class to guess both your animal and your object. Try your descriptions out on your group first. If your descriptions are well and accurately written, the class should be able to guess correctly.

THE TALKING EGGS
Robert D. San Souci
Dial Books for Young Readers, 1989

Charting Stereotypical Characters

The Talking Eggs is a retelling of a folktale from the southern United States. As with many fairy tales, folktales, and even some legends, this one has stereotypical good, evil, and magical characters. In this tale, Blanche is the good character. Rose and her mother are both evil characters, and the old woman is the magical character. Make a chart that has three categories: good, evil, and magical. Using at least 15 to 20 other fairy tales, folktales, and/or legends, find the stereotypical characters in each and list them under the appropriate heading. Be sure to note in which story each character appears.

Writing a Letter

Imagine that you are Blanche. You have gone to the city and are living like a "grand lady." A number of years have passed since you last saw your mother and sister. San Souci says at the end of the book that you are "as kind and generous as always." Write a letter to your mother and sister describing your present life. Will you be kind and generous to them? Place your letter in an envelope and address it. Where will you send it?

Making Fancy Eggs

The plain eggs said, "Take me." The fancy eggs cried, "Don't take me!" What do you think the fancy eggs looked like? Using real eggshells, L'eggs pantyhose containers, styrofoam balls, or something else that is egg-shaped, create a collection of fancy eggs. Choose several different methods to decorate your eggs. Decide on some attractive and artistic way to display your fancy eggs.

TROUBLE RIVER
Betsy Byars
Scholastic, 1969

K. SERVATT

When Indian trouble is feared, Dewey brings his grandmother safely to Hunter City on "his raft, the Rosey B." Dewey rises to the occasion and meets the challenge like a man.

Vocabulary

drone (page 2)
emigrants (page 8)
tuft (page 17)
dusky (page 25)
haunches (page 25)
yonder (page 31)

sluggishly (page 36)
jabbing (page 47)
encrusted (page 48)
maneuver (page 54)
velours (page 59)
satchel (page 59)

reluctantly (page 68)
agonizing (page 76)
frenzied (page 78)
treacherous (page 82)
scalded (page 93)
bedraggled (page 94)

Creating a Three-Dimensional Map

This book takes place sometime during the settling of the American frontier. It is not certain whether Trouble River and Hunter City are real or fictitious. Go to the library and try to find a place like the one described in the book. Create a three-dimensional map of the journey from the cabin to Hunter City via the river. Show Dewey's progress down the river on your map, and pinpoint the specific locations mentioned in the text.

Building a Raft

Make a model of the raft upon which Dewey and Grandma travelled down the river. Try to use the same kinds of materials (or a close facsimile of them) that Dewey used. Be sure the raft floats, and be prepared to demonstrate this to the class.

Planning a Raft Trip

Imagine your family is going to take a rafting vacation. You are responsible for all the planning of the trip. The first thing you'll need to do is find out where this kind of vacation can be taken. Magazines and travel guides from the library can help you find this information. Write to three or four of the most appealing spots and ask for vacation information, pamphlets, and brochures. When you receive all the information, look it over carefully and poll the group members to determine the most desirable vacation spot. Make a chart that shows why you've chosen this particular place over the others. Now you must actually plan the trip. How many people will be going? When will you go? How long will it take to travel to and from the actual rafting location? How will you travel? Will you have to spend the night somewhere along the way? Where will you stay? Will you make reservations? How many meals will you eat before you arrive at your destination? Will you eat in restaurants or take food with you? Do you need to pack any special equipment? Plan your daily itinerary complete with budget.

Building a Sod House

Settlers on the American frontier lived in homes constructed from materials that were readily available to them. The settlers in the area of Trouble River lived in sod homes. Research the construction of a sod home. The two following books by Pam Conrad might help you.

Conrad, Pam. *Prairie Songs*. New York: Harper & Row, 1985.

———. *Prairie Songs: The Life and Times of Solomon Butcher*. New York: HarperCollins, 1991.

Reconstruct a replica of a sod house or one of the outbuildings around the home. Be sure to show some of the surrounding landscape.

Designing a Grandparent Collage

Many poems have been written about grandparents. Look in poetry anthologies to find some of these. After your group looks at these poems, group members should write a poem about one or both of their grandparents. The beginning of the poem might be, "A grandmother is...." or, "A grandfather is...." On a large piece of paper or posterboard, arrange these poems and perhaps a few of your favorites from the anthologies (don't forget to credit all authors) with either photographs of group members' grandparents, pictures of grandparents cut from magazines, or drawings of grandparents. Give your collage an appropriate title.

Designing Your Own Project

If you can think of another project that will clearly demonstrate your knowledge of the text, you may substitute it for one of the projects mentioned above. Talk with your teacher about this.

THERE'S A BOY IN THE GIRLS' BATHROOM
Louis Sachar
Alfred A. Knopf, 1987

K. SERVATT

The teachers say Bradley has many problems, but Carla, the school counselor, likes him. With her help, Bradley learns to like himself and to become accepted by his group of friends.

Vocabulary

bulging (page 4)
asserted (page 16)
lagged (page 56)
confidence (page 78)
baffled (page 119)
unison (page 188)

ceramic (page 10)
gritted (page 18)
romping (page 58)
scoffed (page 85)
dumbfounded (page 131)

flabbergasted (page 15)
gurgling (page 32)
restlessly (page 76)
flailed (page 94)
overwhelmed (page 147)

From *Literature Circles*, 1992. Teacher Ideas Press • P.O. Box 6633 • Englewood, CO 80155-6633.

Telling Bradley's Lies

Bradley Chalkers tells outrageous lies to everyone—his mother, his teacher, his classmates, even his counselor. Make a list of some of the lies Bradley tells. When you share this list with the class, you should be able to tell why you think Bradley told each lie. Discuss possible reasons within your group (you'll probably want to take notes so you don't forget anything in the presentation).

Telling Your Own Lie

Write a true story about something that really happened to you or someone you know well. Insert one (and only one) lie into the story. Read your story to the entire class and challenge them to find the one untruth.

Interviewing the School Counselor

Interview the school counselor. What does the counselor do? How does he/she spend the time at school? Be sure to give an accurate description of Bradley, and then ask the counselor how he/she would try to help Bradley. What kinds of things would he/she do? Has he/she ever met a kid like Bradley? If so, how was the counselor helpful? Generate other questions to ask. You may want to tape-record this interview. If you don't record it, be sure to take accurate notes. Think of an interesting way to present this information to the class. You might do it like an actual interview, with one group member taking the part of the counselor.

Charting Your Choices

In chapter 22 Bradley makes a list of things to talk about with Carla. Choose the ten things on the list that you feel are the most important. Be able to defend your choices. You might want to make a chart that lists your choices and reasons.

Building a Model

Build a three-dimensional model of Bradley's room, his haven in an unsafe world. The animals (Ronnie, Bartholomew, etc.) must be included. Design your own "safe haven." (It's okay if this is your real bedroom.) What would it include? Where would it be located? Either draw or build a model of your safe haven.

Planning a Birthday Party

Bradley goes to Colleen's birthday party—his first birthday party in many years. Design a birthday party that you would give for a picture-book character. You'll need to make invitations, party hats, and party favors (if you feel they're appropriate) and to plan an agenda for the party. Plan a game that some students can play on presentation day. Don't forget the cake! That will be nice to share with the entire class.

Giving a Gift

Each member of the group should do this project individually. You want to give someone a "gift from the heart" as Bradley gave a "gift from the heart" to Carla. Think carefully about this. Who will be the recipient of your gift?

Why did you choose that particular gift? Bring your gift on presentation day, and be prepared to tell why you chose the gift and the recipient.

Designing Your Own Project

If you can think of another project that will clearly demonstrate your knowledge of the book, you may substitute if for one of the projects mentioned above. Talk with your teacher about this.

SNOW TREASURE
Marie McSwigan
E. P. Dutton, 1942

A group of courageous Norwegian boys and girls help their country save its bullion from the German invaders during World War II. Although there is no proof of the truth of the story, it is based on the story told by a ship captain who delivered the gold bullion to Baltimore, Maryland, on June 28, 1940.

Vocabulary

fiords (page 2)
hearth (page 10)
primer (page 17)
blotted (page 31)
trudged (page 41)
rebuked (page 66)
menace (page 115)

tormentor (page 6)
bullion (page 10)
calculation (page 28)
unoffending (page 35)
sepulchres (page 44)
stupor (page 70)

tussle (page 6)
kroner (page 10)
regiment (page 29)
windbreakers (page 40)
camouflage (page 61)
boors (page 106)

From *Literature Circles*, 1992. Teacher Ideas Press • P.O. Box 6633 • Englewood, CO 80155-6633.

Mapping the Story Setting

This story is based on actual events that took place in Riswyk, Norway, during the time of the German invasion at the beginning of World War II. Go to the library and consult an atlas to find Norway and Germany. Locate Oslo and Riswyk, Norway. Locate the Arctic Circle. Draw or construct a map that shows all of the above locations, and label these places. With color or in some other way, indicate the elevations and the climate. Make a key to accompany your map.

Making and Dressing Paper Dolls

Because of the geography, climate, and customs of Norway, the Norwegian style of dress is distinctive. Go to the library and find pictures of and information about the Norwegian people and their clothing. Make paper dolls (you may want to model them after characters in the book). Also make clothes for the dolls that are typically Norwegian. Make outfits that would be suitable for warm weather and outfits that would be suitable for cold weather. Think about how you can present these paper dolls and their clothing to the group. You might "play" one or two scenes from the book.

Sequencing Historical Events

At the time of the German invasion of Norway, on April 8, 1940, conditions in that country were like those of any January (see p. 2). The events described in this book took place in less than three months and helped shape the future of Norway. Make a three-dimensional timeline in the form of a mountainside. Include the village and fiord. Show the events in the order they occurred in the book. Begin with the invasion and end with the deliverance of the gold to Baltimore, Maryland, on June 28, 1940 (see the preface). You might use a sled as an instrument to show movement from one event to another as you present the events in sequence to the entire class on presentation day.

Building a Sled

Make a replica of a sled loaded with gold bricks, like the sleds the children used to carry the gold bullion to the Snake. Materials used are your choice, and the size of the sled should be determined by your group.

Comparing German Occupation of Three Countries

The German army occupied most of the countries in Europe during World War II. In each country people reacted differently to the Nazis. You have read how some of the Norwegian people resisted occupation. The following two books tell how people of two other countries acted toward the Germans during this time.

Innocenti, Roberto. *Rose Blanche*. Mankato, Minn.: Creative Education, 1985.

Lowry, Lois. *Number the Stars*. New York: Dell, 1989.

Rose Blanche is set in Poland, and *Number the Stars* is set in Denmark. Using these two books or others of your choice, along with *Snow Treasure*, compare the ways the citizens reacted to the occupation of their country. Also compare the ways the citizens were treated by the German invaders. Present this information by choosing a representative scene from each book. Act out the scene or present it in readers' theater style.

Writing a Poetic Piece

Imagine you are a child in one of the books you used in the above project. Think about your feelings concerning your situation, your country, your family, and the Nazis. Write a poem that expresses these feelings and publish your poetry in the form of a wall poster. Choose a piece of 11-by-18-inch colored paper. The color should symbolize the emotions represented in the poem. Place your writing attractively on this paper and draw graphics that enhance the meaning of your poetry.

Designing Your Own Project

If you can think of another project that will clearly demonstrate your knowledge of the text, you may substitute it for one of the projects mentioned above. Talk with your teacher about this.

IN THE YEAR OF THE BOAR AND JACKIE ROBINSON
Bette Bao Lord
Harper & Row, 1984

K. SERVATT

Shirley Temple Wong is a Chinese girl who comes to Brooklyn in 1947. When she discovers her love for baseball and the Brooklyn Dodgers, she begins to make friends and feel at home in a strange new land.

Vocabulary

matriarch (page 7)
abacus (page 9)
celestial (page 15)
ebony (page 44)
formidable (page 71)
meticulous (page 111)

dictums (page 7)
festooned (page 14)
queasiness (page 22)
quizzical (page 49)
tyranny (page 102)
berserk (page 143)

buddha (page 9)
courtesans (page 14)
rickshaws (page 28)
gossamer (page 66)
alchemy (page 110)
sterling (page 160)

From *Literature Circles*, 1992. Teacher Ideas Press • P.O. Box 6633 • Englewood, CO 80155-6633.

Charting Chinese and U.S. Customs

The book describes many Chinese customs and beliefs. Find as many of these as you can. Write them down and describe them. Discuss the custom of belief in your group. Is there a similar U.S. custom or belief? If there is, write that down on the same page as its Chinese counterpart. You may want to make a chart that shows the corresponding Chinese and U.S. beliefs or customs to use in your presentation. Here are a few with which to begin.

"Only the aged were considered wise." page 2

"No member of an upright Confucian family ever questioned the conduct of elders." page 2

"It was the season for merrymaking, when the New Year approaches and old debts are paid." page 5

Breaking things during the holidays would "bring bad luck, bad luck for the next three hundred and sixty-five days." page 7

"That was another of Grandmother's dictums. Not a speck of dust. Not a misplaced article. Everything must be in harmony to welcome the New Year." page 7

Symbolizing Shirley's Feelings Artistically

Make an illustrated book of Shirley's feelings and attitudes toward new things she encounters when she moves to the United States. Describe the situation, tell how Shirley felt, and draw a picture or create a collage that either depicts the situation or symbolizes Shirley's feelings about it.

Following Bandit's Life

Make a timeline that follows Bandit's life as she progresses through the story. Be sure to note significant changes such as when she becomes Shirley Temple Wong.

Investigating the Chinese Calendar

The Chinese calendar is much different from the U.S. calendar. For example, the story begins in the Year of the Dog, 4645. In the library, research the Chinese calendar and make a chart that explains it. Why did the author choose the Year of the Boar as the primary focus for this book?

Studying Jackie Robinson

Jackie Robinson was the grandson of a slave and the son of a sharecropper. He was raised by his mother, who took in ironing and washing to earn money. Despite his background, Jackie Robinson went to college, excelled in sports, and served his country in wartime. Why did the author choose to introduce Shirley to the sport of baseball rather than to another sport? Think about the fact that baseball is a team sport and an individual sport. Why did the author choose Jackie Robinson in particular? The text will help you answer these questions. You may want to find out more about Jackie Robinson. Two books that you may find helpful are:

Adler, David. *Jackie Robinson: He Was the First.* New York: Holiday House, 1989.

Cohen, Barbara. *Thank You, Jackie Robinson.* New York: Lothrop, Lee and Shepard Books, 1974.

Choose any form you like to share this information with the class. A poem would work well, as would a combination visual/textual presentation. Or you might do a videotaped television documentary or a radio broadcast.

Predicting the Future

The time is the day after the book ends. Shirley picks up a newspaper and reads her horoscope. What does it say? Use your knowledge of the text and of the character when you predict what Shirley's future will be.

Designing and Building a Kite

Kites have always played an important part in Chinese people's lives. The Chinese word for kite, *feng-cheng*, means wind-harp. The first known use of a kite was by a Chinese general in 200 B.C. He calculated the distance to an enemy fortress by flying a kite over its walls and then measuring the length of string he had used.

Kites originated in China. On the ninth day of the ninth month, the Chinese people celebrate Kite Day. On this day a kite, traditionally made of rice paper or silk stretched over bamboo poles, is set adrift. This special kite is decorated in such a way that it will banish evil spirits. Design and make a kite that will banish evil spirits. You might want to attach your name and address and a note asking the "finder" of your kite to write to you and tell you how far it traveled after you set it adrift.

Designing Your Own Project

If you can think of another project that will clearly demonstrate your knowledge of the text, you may substitute it for one of the projects mentioned above. Talk to your teacher about this.

THE LION, THE WITCH AND THE WARDROBE

C. S. Lewis
Scholastic, 1950

K. SERVATT

First in the *Chronicles of Narnia*, this book tells the story of Lucy, her brothers, and her sister after they accidentally discover the land of Narnia. Their quest is to break the spell of an evil witch who has terrorized the inhabitants of this fantasy land.

Vocabulary

wardrobe (page 5)
melancholy (page 10)
groping (page 25)
fetch (page 35)
bough (page 62)
stratagem (page 73)
spire (page 88)
lithe (page 92)
sluice (page 103)
bristling (page 137)
prodigious (page 165)

glimpse (page 7)
jollification (page 13)
sledge (page 27)
wrenched (page 54)
trifle (page 66)
turret (page 89)
plaguey (page 99)
satyr (page 111)
siege (page 143)
saccharine (page 170)

faun (page 9)
cloven (page 17)
inquisitive (page 32)
crockery (page 54)
oilskin (page 69)
reign (page 78)
centaur (page 92)
curtsey (page 103)
pavilion (page 122)
rabble (page 151)
gibbered (page 174)

From *Literature Circles*, 1992. Teacher Ideas Press • P.O. Box 6633 • Englewood, CO 80155-6633.

Learning about Series

This is Book 1 in a series of books called the *Chronicles of Narnia*, and many of the same characters appear in the books following *The Lion, the Witch and the Wardrobe*. Go to the library and locate a series of picture books. The following list may help you:

Piggins books by Jane Yolen
Commander Toad books by Jane Yolen
Madeline books by Ludwig Bemelmans
Miss Nelson books by Harry Allard
The Magic Schoolbus books by Joanna Cole

Read one of the series and take notes about how the author uses the same characters in different situations. Choose your favorite book in the series to read aloud on presentation day. Make a chart that tells how the main character acts and reacts in different situations in other books in the series.

Making a Timeline

Make a timeline that records the most important events in the book, from the day Lucy looks into the wardrobe until the end of the book when the children come tumbling back into the empty room. You may make the timeline verbal, visual, or a combination of both.

Creating a Travel Brochure

Create a travel brochure to entice visitors to enter Narnia. Make it artistically appealing, colorful, and representative of Narnia in winter and spring. Decide whether or not to include travel costs, means of transportation, and accommodations. Remember that you are trying to sell your audience on taking a journey to a faraway place. Make your advertisement irresistible.

Making a Cartoon Strip

In the book there is a clear struggle between good and evil. There are "good guys" and "bad guys"; good triumphs over evil in the end. Aslan is the protagonist (good guy) of the story. The witch and her cohorts are the antagonists (bad guys). The children support the hero, Aslan. For this activity, invent your own protagonist, antagonist, cast of supporting characters, setting, and plot. Your story should be about good versus evil; good should triumph in the end. Write your story in the form of a cartoon strip. Make your illustrations lively and write the text so it looks like cartoon strips you have read.

Imaging the Hero

Aslan is the hero of the story. Think about the hero of your cartoon strip. Make a large (life-size) image of your hero or heroine. Include enough detail in this image to make your hero or heroine seem real and convincing. Along with this visual representation, make a personality profile that describes your protagonist's personal characteristics. This should be done in such a way that your audience gets a clear idea of what your character looks like and how he or she acts.

Designing Your Own Project

If you can think of another project that will clearly demonstrate your knowledge of the text, you may substitute it for one of the projects mentioned above. Talk with your teacher about this.

MY SIDE OF THE MOUNTAIN
Jean Craighead George
Scholastic, 1959

Great-grandfather Gribley's land in the Catskill Mountains provides young Sam with the opportunity to prove to himself and to his family that he can survive in the woods. He discovers his own resourcefulness and makes friends with many woodland creatures in the process.

Vocabulary

juncos (page 11)
caterpillaring (page 29)
mussels (page 33)
peregrine falcon (page 51)
poacher (page 72)
tubers (page 103)
preen (page 137)

congregate (page 19)
ravines (page 29)
primitive (page 38)
quiver (page 57)
jesses (page 75)
puppish (page 129)
barometer (page 160)

hemlocks (page 21)
boughs (page 30)
dales (page 42)
stroobly (page 57)
sassafras (page 87)
venison (page 131)

From *Literature Circles*, 1992. Teacher Ideas Press • P.O. Box 6633 • Englewood, CO 80155-6633.

Writing Newspaper Articles

You are Matt. Plan and write the first and the last articles that you wrote about Sam, the "wild boy." Be sure that you only use the information you know at the time to write the first article. Incorporate everything you have learned into the last article. Present the articles as if you have clipped them from a newspaper.

Replicating One of Sam's Inventions

The following inventions of Sam's are shown in the book: fish hook (p. 18), leaf bucket (p. 41), game snare (p. 47), and slide willow whistle (p. 100). Choose one of these items or something else that is described but not pictured in the book. Make a replica of your chosen item to explain and demonstrate for the class.

Creating Your Own Special Hideaway

Choose a place near you or some place with which you are familiar (perhaps a place you have visited, a place you have been camping, or a place you have read about). Plan what you would do if you lived there as Sam lived on "his side of the mountain." What would you use for a house? How would you furnish your house? Draw a blueprint or make a tabletop model of your lodging; include the furnishings. Draw a map of your site as Sam did of his. You might want to make your map more detailed than Sam's. Think of a creative way to make a map (perhaps a clay or salt map).

Creating a Symbolistic Collage

Reread the portion of the story that begins on Halloween (pp. 116-20). Why was it significant that these activities took place on Halloween rather than some other holiday? Create a collage that shows what happened and the significance of the date on which the events occurred. As you begin to create your collage, think about colors and what they symbolize. What colors are typically considered Halloween colors? How can you meaningfully incorporate these colors into your collage?

Cooking a Meal to Share

Do you think you could create some of the things Sam ate? Look through the text to see if there are some things we occasionally eat in our homes. How about venison steak, onion soup, fish, and homemade jam? Fix a dish to share with the entire class. A little taste is fine—your classmates won't need a large helping of each dish. If you need to substitute for a few ingredients, that's fine.

Packing a Survival Kit

The time is late spring. Something has happened that will necessitate your living out-of-doors for 10 days with no modern conveniences. You may pack a "survival kit." Your kit may contain no more than 15 items (not including the pack in which you carry them). What will you take and why? You may want to make a chart that lists your survival items. This makes it easier when you explain your project to the class.

Creating a Photo Album

Imagine Sam had a camera with him when he set up housekeeping on "his side of the mountain." Envision the pictures Sam might have taken of himself and his animals and of himself and his few visitors. Draw these "photographs" and put a caption under each one that describes what is happening. Put all the "photos" together into an album.

Designing Your Own Project

If you can think of another project that will clearly demonstrate your knowledge of the text, you may substitute it for one of the projects mentioned above. Talk with your teacher about this.

THE PINBALLS

Betsy Byars
Harper & Row, 1977

K. SERVATT

Carlie says that she, Thomas J., and Harvey are just like "pinballs bouncing from one place to another." Gradually, the three foster children are drawn together as they learn to know and care for each other under the watchful eye of Mr. and Mrs. Mason, their foster parents.

Vocabulary

stabilizes (page 6)
commune (page 24)
appendectomy (page 36)
tottering (page 52)
mutely (page 95)
spigot (page 119)

twinge (page 15)
gnarled (page 25)
boutique (page 43)
wicker (page 80)
decals (page 101)
cameo (page 130)

basin (page 18)
hovered (page 35)
halter (page 45)
respects (page 94)
cahoots (page 114)

From *Literature Circles*, 1992. Teacher Ideas Press • P.O. Box 6633 • Englewood, CO 80155-6633.

Studying Foster Children

Find the Social Services Agency in the telephone book. Arrange to have a speaker come and talk to your group about foster homes and foster children. Be sure to have a list of questions ready to ask the speaker. Some example questions might be:

How does a person become a foster parent?
What are the qualifications they must meet?
Who are foster children?
What eventually becomes of foster children?

You may videotape or tape-record this interview to help you report your information to the entire class in a newspaper format.

Taking a Parenting Poll

To collect opinions from your classmates about "what makes a good parent," prepare a survey that asks them to list qualifications for being a parent. You might ask for five or more qualifications. Distribute these to the classes you have selected (be sure to ask permission from teachers). Tally your results. Compile a list of the top five qualifications and design a parenting license, stating the qualifications somewhere on the license. To earn a license, a prospective parent must pass a test that you have also created. You could write a true/false test, a multiple-choice test, an essay test, or a combination of the three. The license and the accompanying test will be presented to the entire class. You also may choose to administer the test and pass out licenses on presentation day.

Making a Model Room

The author describes various "rooms" where the story unfolds. The boys' bedroom, the Mason's kitchen, and the hospital room are three examples. Using the information in the text, make a three-dimensional model of one of the room in the book. Place the characters who belong in the room in your model. Do this in any way and with any materials you prefer, and make sure your representation is as accurate as possible.

Mapping Three Lives

A life map is a linear representation of a person's life. Curves and places of interest along the way are marked on the map. The curves show the "ups and downs" of that life; the places of interest are marked like cities on a highway. The places of interest are usually shown pictorially with a few words as clues. Map the lives of Carlie, Harvey, and Thomas J. You may choose to do each separately or to intertwine the three as their lives meet. If you do the latter, be sure to code them in some way so a map reader can tell them apart. Color-coding would be one way to distinguish the three. Also, talk in your group about what you think happened to the three characters after the book's end. Map your predictions, too. Designate on the life map(s) where the book ends and where your predictions begin. Place your map(s) on a large enough piece of paper for the entire class to see and follow the progression on presentation day.

Making Puppets

Choose at least three of the characters to portray as puppets. Make a cloth or paper-bag puppet that accurately represents these characters. Pretend you are each character and write about yourself. Remember to write in the first person while describing your life in this story. When you present this to the entire class, you will pretend you are the puppet you are holding.

Writing an Alliterative Book

Alliteration is defined as "the repetition of an initial sound in two or more words of a phrase." For example, "Thomas J. takes too long to water the twins' tall peas" is an alliterative phrase. Write an alliterative book about the characters in *The Pinballs*. Each page should have an illustration and an alliterative phrase. Publish your book properly, with covers, a title page complete with publisher's information, a dedication page, and endpapers.

Designing Your Own Project

If you can think of another project that will clearly demonstrate your knowledge of the book, you may substitute it for one of the projects mentioned above. Talk with your teacher about this.

THE SEARCH FOR DELICIOUS
Natalie Babbitt
Trumpet Club, 1969

K. SERVATT

This delightful fantasy adventure is told in a folktale style. Gaylen is dispatched by the king to find the "best" definition of delicious and succeeds in solving more than one mystery along the way.

Vocabulary

cockatoo (page 13)
ungratified (page 18)
hornbeams (page 26)
undercurrent (page 32)
tranquil (page 42)
chagrin (page 46)
wheezy (page 52)
lute (page 64)
sycamore (page 72)
wheedle (page 80)
brazier (page 101)
hillock (page 111)
derisive (page 129)
zephyr (page 160)

calamitous (page 14)
proclamation (page 24)
jerkin (page 31)
minstrel (page 34)
sapling (page 43)
beadily (page 46)
dispute (page 58)
dismay (page 68)
mobcap (page 73)
gurgled (page 87)
bellows (page 104)
precise (page 120)
resolve (page 131)

flawless (page 18)
poll (page 25)
ear-splitting (page 31)
cobblestones (page 39)
emerged (page 43)
vague (page 52)
grieve (page 60)
primroses (page 72)
gaping (page 77)
southernmost (page 88)
anvil (page 107)
medallion (page 128)
distinguish (page 144)

From *Literature Circles*, 1992. Teacher Ideas Press • P.O. Box 6633 • Englewood, CO 80155-6633.

Locating an Illustrator

This book has very few illustrations, but the text creates pictures in your mind as you read. For this activity, look through picture books and examine the illustrations. Note the different styles of various illustrators. After looking at illustrations in several picture books, decide which illustrator you think could have best done the illustrations for *The Search for Delicious*. Give reasons for your choice. Bring books by that illustrator on the final presentation day. Show sample illustrations and tell why you chose this particular artist.

Writing a Sequel

On the last page of the book, the author seems to suggest that another search may soon begin—a search for "fresh." Using the search for "delicious" as a pattern, write a sequel entitled *The Search for Fresh*. This can be in the form of either a picture book or a wordless picture book. Be sure to use standard book form when publishing your work. You may read your book aloud to the class on presentation day, or you may prepare an audiotape of the book. If you choose to prepare a tape, you'll need background music, an audible sound that signals the time for a page turn, and plenty of "wait" time between pages to allow the audience to look carefully at the illustrations. Lots of practice reading the text orally will help the taping go smoothly.

Making a Chart

Make a chart that shows the events on Gaylen's search for "delicious" and his mission to find Ardis. Also include on the chart what each person considered "delicious." Include the events as told in the prologue and the epilogue.

Surveying Classes

To find out what young people your age consider the most delicious things that exist, compose a survey form that you can have duplicated. Make your survey simple, short, and clear. Pass these forms out to classes in your school. Indicate a deadline for the return of the forms. Graph the results of the survey. Make your graph large and easy for the class to read.

Tasting Delicious Foods

"Delicious" means different things to different people. Prepare a grocery list consisting of some of the "delicious" foods you find mentioned on your survey forms. Decide which foods your group would like to bring to serve on presentation day. Prepare a tray (or trays) of these foods so students are able to sample food that other students find delicious as indicated by the survey. Be sure to plan enough food for everyone.

Designing Your Own Project

If you can think of another project that will clearly demonstrate your knowledge of the text, you may substitute it for one of the projects mentioned above. Talk with your teacher about this.

GONE-AWAY LAKE
Elizabeth Enright
Scholastic, 1957

Portia and Julian, while on a bug-catching expedition, stumble upon tumbledown Victorian houses on the edge of an almost extinct lake. They certainly don't expect the good times and good people they find living there.

Vocabulary

yacht (page 14)
suave (page 35)
pennyroyal (page 52)
damask (page 69)
ulster (page 95)
equipage (page 131)
garrulous (page 181)

garnets (page 29)
cataclysm (page 44)
conch (page 63)
wheedled (page 72)
expostulating (page 119)
crinoline (page 146)

caddis (page 31)
austere (page 48)
arethusas (page 67)
impunity (page 76)
hummocks (page 120)
angelica (page 163)

From *Literature Circles*, 1992. Teacher Ideas Press • P.O. Box 6633 • Englewood, CO 80155-6633.

Making an Illustrated Field Guide

On a leisurely summer hike, Portia and Julian discovered a group of wrecked old houses on the edge of a swamp. Go to the library and find information about plants and animals that live in and around swamps and bogs. Take notes and make sketches including color, size, and shape as you do your research. For your final presentation, describe a swampy or boggy area (called a biome) and the vegetation and wildlife you might find there. Put your description in the form of an illustrated field guide. Use a field guide from the library as a reference to help you decide on a way your book might be put together.

Assembling a Terrarium

Make a terrarium in which you can place plants similar to those described in your field guide. Learn the soil and water requirements of the plants you choose. An aquarium makes a good container for a terrarium, or, for a smaller terrarium, you could use a clean, two-liter plastic bottle. To do this, cut the bottom portion of the plastic bottle right above the dark area. Place the charcoal, soil, and plants in the bottom portion of the bottle and replace the top of the bottle, keeping the lid screwed on the top. If you choose to use an aquarium, be sure to cover it in some way.

Constructing Victorian Houses

Construct one or more Victorian-style houses like the ones that existed on the shores of Gone-Away Lake. You may want to refer to a book in the library that shows architecture from the Victorian era. You might use graham crackers and frosting to create this house, using the following recipe.

ROYAL ICING

Ingredients
2 egg whites (large)
½ teaspoon cream of tartar
3 cups powdered sugar
water as needed
food coloring (optional)

Method
Place the egg whites and cream of tartar in a glass or metal (not plastic) bowl and beat at high speed with hand or electric mixer for 1 minute. Gradually add sugar ¼ cup at a time and continue beating until frosting stands in fluffy peaks. The amount of water needed depends upon the humidity and the purpose for which you need the icing. Protect the icing in the bowl as you work by covering it lightly with a damp towel.

Dressing Up the Characters

When Portia and Julian first saw them, Mrs. Cheever and Mr. Payton must have looked very peculiar and old-fashioned in their Victorian-style clothes. The author creates vivid mental pictures of them with her words. For an example, reread the description of Mrs. Cheever that begins on page 37 and the description of Mr. Payton that begins on page 48. Make a paper doll of each character and make at least two outfits like those described in the story. You may choose to make your paper dolls and their clothing as large as life-size or as small as a regular paper doll. Be sure to make tabs on the paper clothing. Fold these tabs down to keep the articles of clothing on the dolls. Choose any medium (even real fabric) to make your outfits colorful and realistic.

Making Dreams Come True

Portia had hopes of her parents buying and fixing up Villa Caprice for their own. This would be a "dream come true" for her. Add one more chapter of your own to this book to help Portia's dream come true. Illustrations as well as text can tell about events you describe. Make sure you continue by using the author's original style, setting, and characters. Publish this piece simply as chapter 16 of *Gone-Away Lake*. Your final product could range from book size to mural size; it could be handheld or free-standing.

Designing Your Own Project

If you can think of another project that will clearly demonstrate your knowledge of the book, you may substitute it for one of the other projects. Talk with your teacher about this.

HONEY GIRL
Madge Harrah
Avon Books, 1990

K. SERVATT

Young Dorothy, one of a family of beekeepers, travels on a barge down the Mississippi River. The adventures of the family, as the travel from the cold climes of Wisconsin to the warmth of Arkansas, are enchanting, witty, and courageous. The story is based on a true account of a trip taken by the Stahmann family, famous for their pecan plantations in southern New Mexico and Australia.

Vocabulary

awning (page 2)	pelted (page 8)	freshwater pearls (page 16)
iridescent (page 18)	slugs (page 22)	determination (page 43)
slate (page 45)	currents (page 46)	snags, deadheads, wing dams (page 53)
derelicts (page 57)	bluffs (page 62)	shanty boat (page 73)
lock (page 82)	ragamuffins (page 90)	slough (page 105)

From *Literature Circles*, 1992. Teacher Ideas Press • P.O. Box 6633 • Englewood, CO 80155-6633.

47

Finding and Rewriting Similes

A simile is a figure of speech that likens one thing to another by the use of *like* or *as*. The author uses many similes in *Honey Girl*. For example, on page 103, she says, "The barge charged forward, pushing the pole straight up into the air and carrying Dorothy with it like a cat clinging to a tree trunk." Find other places (at least five) in the novel where the author uses a simile. Copy down each simile, and then rewrite the line without using the simile. "The barge charged forward, pushing the pole straight up into the air and carrying Dorothy with it," is one way the example simile could be rewritten. The meaning of the sentence doesn't change. Why do you think Harrah uses similes so extensively? How do similes enhance readers' enjoyment of a book?

Designing a Book Cover

Madge Harrah is both the author and the illustrator of *Honey Girl*. The illustration on the cover of the book, however, is not the one that Harrah designed. Also, *Honey Girl* was not the title that the author had chosen. Imagine you are Madge Harrah. Design the cover for the book remembering that both the title and the illustration will be different. Look carefully at Harrah's illustrations when planning your cover.

Taking a Train Trip

After living in Arkansas for a year, the Stahmann family moved by train to the El Paso, Texas, area. What were trains like in the early 1900s? What route would the train have taken from Arkansas to El Paso? How long would the trip have taken? Draw a picture of the train Dorothy and her family might have ridden. Make a map and chart the course the train would have followed. Be sure to include the stops the train would have made. Imagine you are Dorothy, and write diary entries that tell the story of the trip.

Growing and Cooking with Pecans

Deane Stahmann founded Stahmann Farms, Inc., a pecan plantation in the Las Cruces, New Mexico, area. How are the nuts grown? Why do you think the Stahmanns chose Australia as the location for their second pecan plantation? Study the effects of pesticides on the food we eat and on the environment. Randy Stahmann has been nationally recognized for his use of ladybugs in controlling aphids. How does this work? Is it important that growers move away from pesticides to natural controls? Why or why not? Find and prepare a recipe that includes pecans. Make enough for everyone in the class to have a taste. As you pass out the food, tell what you have learned about the Stahmanns.

Telling a Legend

Two legends are told in the book: the legend of the Indian maiden in Lake Pepin and the legend of Paul Bunyan and his blue ox, Babe. Many legends and folktales surround the history of the people of North America. Find a legend or folktale that intrigues you and either read or tell it to the entire class. The following titles might interest you.

Anaya, Rudolfo A. *The Farolitos of Christmas*. Santa Fe, N.M.: *New Mexico Magazine*, 1987.

Harper, Wilhelmina. *The Gunniwolf*. New York: Trumpet Club, 1989.

Hayes, Joe. *La Llorona—The Weeping Woman*. El Paso, Tex.: Cinco Puntos Press, 1987.

Hooks, William H. *The Ballad of Belle Dorcas*. New York: Alfred A. Knopf, 1990.

San Souci, Robert D. *The Legend of Scarface*. New York: Doubleday, 1978.

_____. *Song of Sedna*. New York: Doubleday, 1981.

The Talking Eggs. New York: Dial Books for Young Readers, 1989.

Finding the Governing Word

The word *patience* seemed to be the governing force in Dorothy's life. Make a list of 10 important historical figures, well-known fictional characters, or a combination of both. Tell what the governing word in their lives would have been, and be ready to explain your choice.

Designing Your Own Project

If you can think of another project that will clearly demonstrate your knowledge of the text, you may substitute it for one of the projects listed above. Talk with your teacher about this.

JULIE OF THE WOLVES
Jean Craighead George
Trumpet Club, 1972

K. SERVATI

Set in three different parts of Alaska, this book tells the story of Miyax (known as Julie to her pen pal in San Francisco) who runs away from Daniel, her child-husband, and her home in Barrow only to find herself lost in the Alaskan wilderness. Her eventual acceptance by an Arctic wolf pack ensures her survival as she gradually comes to terms with the reality of Eskimo life.

Vocabulary

Arctic ground squirrels (page 7)
Lapland longspurs (page 9)
sandpiper (page 10)
snowy owl (page 14)
caribou (page 14)
Arctic pea (page 30)

polar bears (page 8)
crane fly (page 9)
lemming (page 13)
weasel (page 14)
wolves (page 18)
sedge (page 43)

moss, grass, lichens (page 9)
puffin (page 10)
white fox (page 14)
siskin (page 14)
jaeger (page 29)
bunting (page 45)

From *Literature Circles*, 1992. Teacher Ideas Press • P.O. Box 6633 • Englewood, CO 80155-6633.

Mapping the Area

Miyax grew up in and around Barrow, Alaska, near the Arctic Circle, and she traveled to Kangik on the Bering Sea. Go to the library and trace a map of this area. Locate and label the above places. Find information about the Inuit people (*National Geographic* magazines are a good source). Take notes for your final presentation, when you will talk about the Inuit people as you point out on the map where they live.

Making a Wolf Communication Chart

By observing wolf behavior, Julie was able to survive when she became lost on the Arctic tundra. She became aware of their intricate system of communication using body language and howling. Make a Wolf Communication Chart that shows or tells what messages are sent by the wolves and what each message means. This information may be found in your book or in one of the following books.

Andrews, Julia L. *Wolves.* New York: Trumpet Club, 1990.

Brett, Jan. *The First Dog.* San Diego, Calif.: Harcourt Brace Jovanovich, 1988.

George, Jean Craighead. *The Wounded Wolf.* New York: Harper & Row, 1978.

Hansen, Rosanna. *Wolves and Coyotes.* New York: Platt and Munk, 1981.

Hughes, Ted. *Wolfwatching.* New York: Farrar, Straus & Giroux, 1991.

Johnson, Sylvia A., and Alice Aamodt. *Wolf Pack, Tracking Wolves in the Wild.* Minneapolis, Minn.: Lerner Publications, 1985.

Lawrence, R. D. *In Praise of Wolves.* New York: Henry Holt, 1984.

Mech, David L. *The Wolf: The Ecology and Behavior of an Endangered Species.* Garden City, N.Y.: Natural History Press, 1970.

Mowat, Farley. *Never Cry Wolf.* Boston: Little, Brown, 1963.

Pringle, Laurence P. *Wolfman: Exploring the World of Wolves.* New York: Scribner, 1983.

Savage, Candace. *Wolves.* San Francisco: Sierra Club Books, 1988.

Wexo, John Bonnett. *Wolves.* Mankato, Minn.: Creative Education, 1990.

Creating a Mural

Make a mural in three parts depicting the way the book was organized—in three parts. You may choose to organize the sequence using "flashback" as the book does, or you may decide to show the sequence of events as they actually happened. Create your mural with whatever medium your group decides is the most effective and appropriate.

Constructing an Inuit Ice House

Using sugar cubes, construct an Inuit ice house like the one described in the third part of the book. Present it in an appealing manner. You may need to refer again to the *National Geographic* magazines in your library.

Designing a Book of Arctic Animals

Make an illustrated "Book of Arctic Animals." These animals are mentioned in *Julie of the Wolves.* Make an attractive cover for your book and include a title page and endpapers. On each page, have either a drawn or cut-out picture of each animal, the name of the animal, and a short description of the animal. Include the following animals:

wolves (p. 18)	Arctic ground squirrels (p. 7)
polar bear (p. 8)	Lapland longspurs (p. 9)
crane fly (p. 9)	bunting (p. 45)
puffin (p. 10)	sandpiper (p. 10)
lemming (p. 13)	white fox (p. 14)
snowy owl (p. 14)	weasel (p. 14)
jaeger (p. 29)	siskin (p. 14)
caribou (p. 14, 55)	Arctic tern (p. 43)
walrus (p. 51)	musk ox (p. 51)
eider (p. 52)	squaw ducks (p. 62)
seal (p. 76)	

Interviewing Julie

Imagine that Julie eventually goes to live and attends school in San Francisco. She becomes a zoologist, and her life's work is to preserve the wolf and its habitat. Imagine you are a television newscaster, and you have been given the job of interviewing Julie for the evening news. Write the questions you will ask and the answers Julie will give. You may videotape this interview and show it for your final presentation, or you may conduct a live TV interview. Some topics your questions and answers might cover are:

social structure of wolf packs

solo wolves

wolf range and territory

wolf communication

wolf recovery

radio tracking

hunting of wolves

The books mentioned on page 51 are good sources of information.

Carving Arctic Animals

The Inuit people are famous for their soapstone carvings of Arctic animals. Using bars of soap, make carvings of Arctic animals mentioned in the book. Decide on an attractive way to display and label these carvings.

Designing Your Own Project

If you can think of another project that would clearly demonstrate your knowledge of the book, you may substitute it for one of the above projects. Talk with your teacher about this.

OLD YELLER
Fred Gipson
Scholastic, 1956

Travis and his big "yeller" dog face many dangers, adventures, and humorous situations together while Travis is the "man of the house" during his father's absence. Little does he realize how attached he has become to the dog and how grateful he is to Yeller for his family's safety until he is faced with the decision of having to destroy the animal.

Vocabulary

varmints (page 3)
middling meat (page 14)
briars (page 41)
riled (page 48)
tushes (page 77)

depredations (page 4)
javelina (page 17)
gobbler (page 42)
rogue (page 50)
entrails (page 86)

frazzle (page 12)
clamoring (page 24)
hydrophobia (page 46)
balked (page 76)

From *Literature Circles*, 1992. Teacher Ideas Press • P.O. Box 6633 • Englewood, CO 80155-6633.

Tracing the Route of the Cattle Drive

The book takes place someplace in Texas. Using clues given in the text and information found in an atlas in the library, decide where in Texas you think the family lived. Draw a map of this place and trace the route the father probably would have taken to get the steers to Abilene, Kansas. You might want to look for some information on the Chisolm Trail to help you decide on the route for the cattle drive.

Creating a Pictorial Chart

When Old Yeller arrives at the farm, Travis does not like the big, yellow dog. What incidents happen that change Travis's mind about the dog? Make a list of the incidents that endear Old Yeller to Travis and the rest of the family. Also, as you read, make a list of occurrences that you think help Travis to mature or "grow up" and to take full responsibility for the welfare of his family while his father is absent. Can you see a correlation between the two lists? Create some kind of pictorial chart, diagram, or panelled mural that shows how Old Yeller helped Travis to mature.

Investigating Hydrophobia

What is hydrophobia? A description of the disease begins on page 63 in the text. What is the name used for hydrophobia today? Is the disease still present in today's society? Make a film documentary (it may be videotaped or done "live") that explains hydrophobia. Besides using information found in the library, you may want to consult a local veterinarian, the animal control center in your area, or the Humane Society. When preparing your documentary, don't forget that you will need some kind of visual enhancement for your verbal text.

Interviewing Sam Houston and Santa Ana

The book is set immediately following the Civil War. The first chapter tells of some of the safeguards that were set in place to help the people who had come to settle in this new and still wild land. For years Texas had been a battleground for people from the United States and the Mexican people. Tell of some of the struggles that occurred in Texas in the early 1800s. Look for information on Sam Houston, Texas's first president and also its first governor, and on Houston's greatest adversary, the Mexican general Santa Ana. How was the Texas-Mexico problem solved? Was there still a problem in the late 1860s when the book took place? Present this information in the form of a dialogue between Sam Houston and Santa Ana. Choose one member of your group to be each character. You might want to choose another group member to be an interviewer.

Dealing with Grief

Travis deals with his grief over the loss of Old Yeller in a very normal way. Most people go through four stages when dealing with a loss of a loved one. One book that describes these stages in a simple, yet very informative way is the following:

Clifton, Lucille. *Everett Anderson's Goodbye.* New York: Henry Holt, 1983.

Read this book or another you can find that describes the four stages of grief. Looking at the last chapter of the novel, find places where you think Travis goes through each stage. Make an informational chart that describes each stage and shows the correlation to the book.

Making a Visual Representation

On page 74 Travis describes two places that he especially likes. Using any kind of art form you prefer, create a representation of one of these places or any other that you find particularly appealing.

Designing Your Own Project

If you can think of another project that will clearly demonstrate your knowledge of the text, you may substitute it for one of the projects described above. Talk with your teacher about this.

NUMBER THE STARS

Lois Lowry
Dell, 1989

During the World War II German occupation of Denmark, the Danes were ingenious in finding ways to transport their Jewish citizens to safety. This story, based on fact, tells how one family helped another escape the Nazi threat.

Vocabulary

dawdled (page 18)
imperious (page 39)
ruefully (page 69)
mourning (page 77)
urgency (page 81)
warily (page 120)

synagogue (page 35)
unwavering (page 48)
specter (page 69)
trudged (page 78)
encased (page 89)
permeated (page 136)

rabbi (page 35)
exasperation (page 57)
deftly (page 75)
sulking (page 78)
winced (page 101)

From *Literature Circles*, 1992. Teacher Ideas Press • P.O. Box 6633 • Englewood, CO 80155-6633.

Mapping the Route

The situation in Denmark during World War II was very much like the situation described in the book. The Danes really did smuggle Jewish people into Sweden, literally under the "noses" of the Germans. Go to the library and find a map of the Scandinavian countries. Draw a map and trace the path the Danish fishing boats traveled to take the Jews to Sweden.

Making a Timeline

Make a timeline that shows Annemarie's life throughout the text. Keep this up to date as the group meets each day to discuss the reading.

Showing Your Family Photographs

The time is 20 years after the book has ended. You are Annemarie. A visitor has come to your home and asked about the time during the war. The visitor wants to know about your family, then and now. He also wants to know about the Rosens. Bring out your family photo album to help you tell the story to the visitor. To make the photo album, you may use real photographs, pictures from magazines, or drawings. Make it seem as authentic as possible. Be prepared to tell the story as you show the pictures. You'll need to think about all the things that have happened in the last 20 years. How has each member of the family changed? What is each person doing now? Where are you living? Look at your own family's photos to see what kinds of things to include.

Writing a Letter

You are Ellen. The time is shortly after you were smuggled into Sweden (you must decide the exact time). Write a letter to Annemarie. Tell her about the voyage, who met you when you arrived in Sweden, and where you are living and with whom. Have you been reunited with the rest of your family? Assume this is the only letter that will reach Annemarie until the end of the war; it will not fall into the hands of the Germans.

Interviewing Rose and Annemarie

Read the picture book *Rose Blanche* by Roberto Innocenti. How are Rose and Annemarie alike? How are they different? Innocenti shows many changes in mood and feelings through his illustrations. How does he accomplish this? How does Lowry show the same kinds of changes with words? Cite specific examples from the text. Compare Rose's fate to Ellen's fate. Why were their fates so different? Use an interview situation when presenting this project. The authors or the characters may be the subjects of the interviews. Prepare your questions and answers carefully. They should be based on the knowledge you have acquired through the comparison and contrast of characters and authors' methods of presentation. You may use a videotaped presentation or you may present it live. Read *Rose Blanche* aloud to the entire class before presenting the interview so everyone will understand what you are doing.

Innocenti, Roberto. *Rose Blanche*. Mankato, Minn.: Creative Education, 1985.

Charting Differences in Holidays

Much of this book centers around Jewish beliefs, customs, and holidays. Your understanding of the book will be much greater if you know more about the Jewish religion. The following books will help you.

Chaikin, Miriam. *Sound the Shofar*. New York: Clarion Books, 1986.

Cone, Molly. *The Jewish New Year*. New York: Thomas Y. Crowell, 1966.

Drucker, Malka. *Rosh Hashana and Yom Kippur—Sweet Beginnings.* New York: Holiday House, 1981.

Greenfeld, Howard. *Rosh Hashana and Yom Kippur.* New York: Holt, Rinehart & Winston, 1979.

The text speaks specifically about the Jewish New Year, Rosh Hashana. Find out what Rosh Hashana is, how it is celebrated, and what special items are used in the celebration. Think about how American non-Jews celebrate the New Year. Make a chart that compares the celebration of the Jewish New Year to the celebration of the January 1 New Year.

Designing Your Own Project

If you can think of another project that will clearly demonstrate your knowledge of the text, you may substitute it for one of the projects mentioned above. Talk with your teacher about this.

THE GREAT GILLY HOPKINS

Katherine Paterson
Avon Flare, 1983

Gilly meets her match in Mrs. Trotter, her latest in a long list of foster mothers. Through trust and unconditional love, Mrs. Trotter prepares Gilly for the reality of going to live with her mother and grandmother.

Vocabulary

fanatic (page 13)

louse nit (page 43)

measly (page 65)

reluctantly (page 87)

belligerently (page 125)

gosling (page 18)

leering (page 46)

steadfastly (page 79)

woolly mammoth (page 89)

fracas (page 24)

strategy (page 49)

massive (page 81)

faltering (page 111)

From *Literature Circles*, 1992. Teacher Ideas Press • P.O. Box 6633 • Englewood, CO 80155-6633.

Learning about Foster Homes

Go to the library and find out about foster homes. What is a foster home? Who lives in one? What kind of people take in foster children? Arrange through the Social Services Agency in your area to have a speaker come talk to your group. Using the information you have learned about foster homes, families, and children, prepare a list of questions you want to ask your guest. You may videotape this interview for presentation to the entire class, or you may want to report the information using a newspaper format.

Finding Similarities and Differences

Gilly and Mrs. Trotter both had expectations for themselves and for each other. Make four lists:

1. Gilly's expectations for herself

2. Gilly's expectations for Mrs. Trotter

3. Mrs. Trotter's expectations for herself

4. Mrs. Trotter's expectations for Gilly

Are there any similarities in these lists? Create a chart or diagram that shows the similarities and/or differences. You might want to use a color-coding system to identify the characters. Be mindful that the expectations will change as the story progresses.

Rapping about Characters

Create a rap based on the main characters in the novel. Rap usually conforms to the following format:

Rap is made up of stanzas.
Each stanza is four lines long.
Each line in the stanza has two beats.
The first and third lines in the stanza do not rhyme.
The second and fourth lines in the stanza do rhyme.

Example:

Here I come
Ready or not
Gilly's my name
I'm a real hot shot

Compose a few verses for each character. When you present the rap, you'll need to dress up like the character you represent, create a life-size replica of that character, make a life-size dummy of the character, or find another way to show the entire class what the character actually looked like.

Surveying Parents and Children

Make a "parent license." To find out the qualifications of a good parent, you'll need to conduct a survey. You may want to include parents as well as children. The survey should take one of two forms: (1) ask the participants to name three or four qualifications of a good parent or (2) create a written survey in which participants note with which qualifications they agree. Using either a bar or a circle graph, chart your results. Make a certificate, suitable for framing, that could be given to parents who meet the qualifications deemed most important in your survey. Could you give a certificate to your parents?

Writing a Last Chapter

The story ends as Gilly goes with her mother and grandmother. Write one more chapter for the book. The form the chapter takes is up to you. It could be an epilogue, a letter to Trotter or W. E., or a chapter written in narrative form. Tell what happens to Gilly. As the author has done in the previous chapters, be sure to tell how Gilly feels about the new happenings in her life and how she deals with them. You may want to mail your new ending to the author, Katherine Paterson. If you choose to do this, mail it to her in care of the publisher. She will probably write back to you. She is very interested in how young people feel about her books.

Designing Your Own Project

If you can think of another project that will clearly demonstrate your knowledge of the text, you may substitute it for one of the projects mentioned above. Talk with your teacher about this.

THE DOOR IN THE WALL

Marguerite de Angeli
Scholastic, 1949

The beautiful language of the text carries the reader along on Robin's journey to Castle Lindsay to meet his father, who is fighting the Scots in the north, and his mother, who is travelling with the queen. Brother Luke teaches Robin to be strong in spite of his useless legs so that he is ready and able to take advantage when "the door in the wall" appears. English life in the Middle Ages is authentically described.

Vocabulary

mailed (page 7)
porridge (page 10)
plague (15)
friar (page 16)
monasteries (page 19)
tonsured (page 31)
pasty (page 52)
turret (page 78)
bailey (page 85)
coif (page 117)

shire reeve (page 9)
victuals (page 11)
cloister (page 15)
jennet (page 17)
scriptorium (page 23)
missal (page 38)
abbot (page 64)
fripperies (page 84)
priory (page 100)

putrid (page 9)
hospice (page 12)
pallets (page 15)
breviary (page 18)
parchment (page 23)
galled (page 51)
heath (page 73)
portcullis (page 85)
sacristan (page 104)

From *Literature Circles*, 1992. Teacher Ideas Press • P.O. Box 6633 • Englewood, CO 80155-6633.

Making a Map

The United Kingdom (U.K.) consists of England, Scotland, Wales, and Northern Ireland. Go to the library and consult an atlas. Locate London, England, where the book begins. Then find the Welsh border (between Wales and England), near which was Castle Lindsay. Make a map showing the United Kingdom. Locate and label the places mentioned above. Your map may be traced or drawn freehand, or you may choose to present this part of the world in a more creative and innovative way.

Charting Life in the Middle Ages

This book takes place during the Middle Ages. You have learned much from your reading about life in this time period. For example, foods, methods of transportation, styles of dress, kinds of shelter, types of occupations, recreational activities, and dangers encountered while travelling are mentioned throughout the book. Go to the library and find supplemental information about everyday life in the Middle Ages. Take notes on your research. Using these notes and information from the book, arrange everything you have learned in categories. Compare each aspect of life in the Middle Ages to life today. For example, one category might be transportation. In the Middle Ages people travelled by boat, horse, or wagon or on foot. Today people travel by boat, plane, train, motorcycle, or bicycle or on foot. Present your information. Draw pictures or cut pictures from magazines to enhance your presentation.

Creating a Book of Illuminations

In the Middle Ages parchment was used for writings rather than paper. To keep from wasting any space on the parchment, the monks did not skip to the next page to start a new chapter. Instead, they showed where a new chapter began by making the first letter of the first word in a chapter very large and fancy. These elaborate letters were often made with gold leaf, and they were called illuminations. Make a book of illuminations using the first letters of the names of at least five of the characters in the book. On each page write a sentence about one character, beginning with the character's name. (See page 23 in the text.) Illustrate the page on which the sentence appears. Make a cover or a title page and a table of contents for your book. Put all of your pages together in book form.

Designing Your Coat-of-Arms

A coat-of-arms is a pictorial representation of a family's ancestry, occupation, and station in life. During the Middle Ages families of importance used coats-of-arms to identify themselves in many ways. The design was frequently embroidered on cloth or publicly displayed in other ways. On page 114 in the text, coats-of-arms appear on flags. Create a book of heraldry that consists of coats-of-arms designed by at least three group members. These coats-of-arms should represent their family characteristics. They may be drawn, painted, stitched, or done in any other original manner. They should be organized in a book of heraldry to present to the class.

Building a Castle

Castle Lindsay and the surrounding countryside is shown on pages 122 and 123. Construct a castle using Castle Lindsay as a model. You may use cardboard (paper-towel rolls, toilet-paper rolls, plastic-wrap rolls), sugar cubes, blocks, or any material of your choice. Make your castle on some kind of platform so it can be moved. Detail the surrounding countryside on the platform. The following book is a good resource:

Macaulay, David. *Castle.* Boston: Houghton Mifflin, 1977.

Designing Your Own Project

If you can think of another project that will clearly demonstrate your knowledge of the book, you may substitute it for one of the other projects mentioned above. Talk with your teacher about this.

CHARLEY SKEDADDLE
Patricia Beatty
Troll Associates, 1987

K. SERVATT

"Skedaddle" is just what Charlie did when he saw the rebel soldier fall. Only 12 years old, Charley leaves New York City and the Bowery Boys to join the 140th Regiment of the Union Army. Granny Bent, who lives high in the Appalachian Mountains, discovers Charley hiding in her chicken coop. She takes him into her home and teaches him to stay rather than skedaddle.

Vocabulary

omnibuses (page 2)
greatcoat (page 18)
haversack (page 26)
ratamacus (page 62)
array (page 76)
conscriptors (page 102)
visored (page 137)

incorrigible (page 11)
regiment (page 19)
recruit (page 32)
pontoons (page 71)
recriminations (page 91)
sassafras (page 113)
caterwauling (page 157)

pungent (page 16)
bulkhead (page 21)
blarney (page 48)
courier (page 72)
hardtack (page 100)
gristmill (page 120)
fodder (page 167)

From *Literature Circles*, 1992. Teacher Ideas Press • P.O. Box 6633 • Englewood, CO 80155-6633.

Researching the Civil War

This book takes place at the end of the Civil War (1864-1865). Charley left his New York City home to join the 140th Regiment of the Union Army. He fought in the Battle of the Wilderness and then found refuge in the Blue Ridge Mountains. Go to the library and find out when and where the Civil War took place. Find out about the Union and Confederate armies. Who fought in these armies? Who were the leaders for each? Who were generals Ulysses S. Grant, George Meade, and Robert E. Lee? Why was this war fought? Using the notes you have taken in the library, create a dialogue among the three generals. This should take place after the war and should be reminiscent of the battles discussed in the text. You may present your dialogue as a conversation, an interview (it must be live—there was no TV then), an interview in the newspaper, or any other creative way your group can think of.

Tracing Charley's Route

Make a topographical map of the area described in the book. Trace Charley's route from New York City, to Culpeper, to the Battle of the Wilderness, and west to the Blue Ridge Mountains in Virginia. Label each of these locations. You may choose to make a map of the entire United States, designating these places in relation to the rest of the country, or you may choose to make a large map of only this area of the United States. You can decide how to make your map, and some suggestions for materials to use are clay, papier-mâché, or salt dough. If you choose the last, remember that the dough takes several days to dry before it can be painted.

Making a Historical Timeline

Make a timeline that shows the events that took place in the book. Include important historical facts that are mentioned both in the text and in the author's notes (p. 181). You may choose to make a one-dimensional or a three-dimensional display of this information. Use pictorial representations to add interest to your timeline.

Writing a Eulogy

"Skedaddle" was the name given to Charley Quinn because he deserted the Union Army and ran away to the Blue Ridge Mountains. Imagine that Charley returned to Jerusha Bent's mountain and lived 40 more years. When he died, you were asked to give the eulogy at his funeral. You want to rename Charley because the name Skedaddle no longer is appropriate. Write this eulogy for Charley (new name), and then design and make a suitable tombstone for his grave. You may choose your materials to do this.

Re-creating Appalachian Folk Art

Appalachian mountain people are famous for their folk art. If you were to travel through the Blue Ridge Mountains, you might find for sale homemade quilts, braided rugs, brooms, baskets, wood carvings, wooden toys and decoys, cornhusk dolls, dried-apple dolls, and musical instruments. Find pictures of some of this folk art in books such as the following.

Bourgeois, Paulette. *The Amazing Apple Book.* Reading, Mass.: Addison-Wesley, 1990.

Panyella, August. *Folk Art of the Americas.* New York: Holt, Rinehart & Winston, 1979.

For this activity, re-create one or more of these examples of Appalachian folk art. Of course, you are not expected to be an expert craftsperson. Simply do the best job you can when working on your project. You will be pleased to discover just how talented you can be. Your group may choose to do one project that you find appealing, or more than one project may be done within your group. When your folk art is completed, find a pleasing way to display your work.

Designing Your Own Project

If you can think of another project that will clearly demonstrate your knowledge of the text, you may substitute it for one of the projects mentioned above. Talk with your teacher about this.

SING DOWN THE MOON

Scott O'Dell
Laurel-Leaf Books, 1970

She has survived capture by the Spanish slavers, but Bright Morning's greatest challenge is yet to come. The author provides insight into Navajo life as Bright Morning and her people are forced to march to Fort Sumner, New Mexico, in the 1860s.

Vocabulary

barrancas (page 8)
hogan (page 22)
tortillas (page 45)
buckskin (page 65)
buttress (page 98)

mesa (page 11)
camisa (page 34)
Penitentes (page 47)
yucca root (page 67)

Long Knives (page 20)
baile (page 41)
mesquite (page 49)
crone (page 91)

From *Literature Circles*, 1992. Teacher Ideas Press • P.O. Box 6633 • Englewood, CO 80155-6633.

67

Mapping the Locations of the Story

The story has three settings: Canyon de Chelly, Arizona; Mexico; and Fort Sumner, New Mexico (Bosque Redondo). Go to the library and consult an atlas to locate these places. Find pictures of Canyon de Chelly. Discuss what you think the land is like in this area. Why do you think the land is prized by the Navajos? Part of the book is about that part of Navajo history called the "Long Walk." Trace the distance between Canyon de Chelly and Fort Sumner. Using the map scale, calculate the distance from one to the other. Find information about the Long Walk (the Fearing Time). In what year did it take place? Do you think the Long Knives were correct to do what they did? Make a large map that shows the three settings of the story. Be prepared to answer all of the above questions as you show and describe the map to the entire class on the final presentation day.

Making a Navajo ABC Dictionary

The words listed in the vocabulary section have special meaning to the Navajo people. Add to this list so there is one word for each of the letters of the alphabet. Alphabetize the words and make an ABC dictionary of the words you have chosen. Be sure to highlight in some way the beginning letter of each word. Determine a creative way to define and illustrate each word.

Drawing Bright Morning's Life

A "life map" is like a map of a trip. However, instead of places being mapped, events in someone's life are charted. Use pictures to describe the route of Bright Morning's life. Take special notice of the good and bad things that happen to her. These are often called the "ups and downs" of life. Knowing this might help you plot your map on a large piece of paper. Use verbal clues along with each picture to help the class follow the course of Bright Morning's life.

Sketching a Panelled Mural

The Chinese often use panels to create three different scenes in one picture. To see how this is done, look at some books that were illustrated by Ed Young.

Louie, Ai-Ling. *Yeh-Shen*. New York: Philomel Books, 1982.

Young, Ed. *Lon Po Po*. New York: Philomel Books, 1989.

Sketch a mural of your own that shows the three different settings in the book. Experiment with some new art techniques: pastels, watercolor wash, or three-dimensional paper affixed to the mural.

Weaving a Navajo Blanket

Many good books in the library tell about weaving, weaving tools, and the weaving process. Particularly informative is the following:

Znamierowski, Nell. *Step-by-Step Weaving*. New York: Golden Press, 1967.

The Navajos, when weaving their patterns into rugs or blankets, always put a "break" in the pattern so the spirit of the weaver could escape. If there were no "break," the spirit of the weaver would be held by the piece, and the weaver would not be able to weave again.

Make a loom and weave a small rug or blanket. You may imitate a Navajo pattern or create a pattern of your own. Be sure to have a "break" in the pattern to let your spirit escape.

Finding Out about Navajos Today

If Bright Morning were living today, things would be very different for her. For information about Navajo schools and jobs for teenagers, write to: Navajo Tribal Council, c/o Navajo Agency, Window Rock, Arizona 86515. After you receive information back from the agency, write about what you think Bright Morning would be doing today. You may choose to write in prose or poetry form.

Designing Your Own Project

If you can think of another project that will clearly demonstrate your knowledge of the text, you may substitute it for one of the projects mentioned above. Talk with your teacher about this.

ISLAND OF THE BLUE DOLPHINS

Scott O'Dell
Laurel-Leaf Books, 1978

K. SERVATT

Karana's Pacific island lies "like a dolphin in the sun." An Indian girl survives alone on the island. She overcomes the weather, wild dogs, and hunger. Based on fact, the story describes the life of a girl, the Lost Woman of San Nicolas, who lived on the island for 18 years.

Vocabulary

cormorant (page 10)
ravine (page 12)
awl (page 42)
sandspit (page 52)
trinkets (page 59)
crevice (page 63)

kelp (page 11)
pelt (page 28)
pitched (page 44)
headland (page 57)
sinew (page 62)
fiber (page 71)

cove (page 12)
abalone (page 33)
nettles (page 51)
league (page 57)
cholla bush (page 63)
chafing (page 73)

From *Literature Circles*, 1992. Teacher Ideas Press • P.O. Box 6633 • Englewood, CO 80155-6633.

Investigating the Location

In the Pacific Ocean, 75 miles southwest of Los Angeles, California, lies an island that looks like a big fish sunning itself in the sea. This island, San Nicolas Island, is the setting of this book. Far to the north is a group of islands, southwest of Alaska, called the Aleutian Islands. Go to the library and consult an atlas to locate these islands. Draw a map that shows their location. Why do you think the Aleuts chose to come to Karana's island? Why did the Aleuts want to take home so many sealskins? What are the major differences between Karana's island and the Aleutian Islands? Use an encyclopedia to find information about the Aleutian Islands to answer these questions. Take notes so you will be prepared to share the information with the whole class during your final presentation.

Writing a Letter

It is two years since the end of the book. Write a letter to the readers of *Island of the Blue Dolphins*. Using the first person, tell what you (Karana) have been doing since the ship picked you up. Now that you have had time to reflect, how do you feel about the time you spent alone on the island? If you could do it all over again, knowing what you know now, would you spend your time any differently?

Creating a Relief Map

Create a relief map out of clay, papier-mâché, or salt dough showing the island, its prominent features, and the surrounding water. Use descriptions found in the book as a guide.

Weaving with Plants or Grasses

Using plants or grasses that grow in your area, weave a basket such as Karana might have used, a skirt that could be like her yucca skirt (p. 47), a mat like one she might have used for sleeping, a hut and fence like those Karana built for shelter and protection (pp. 79-84), or any other pertinent item Karana both made and used.

Making an Island Collage

Make a collage showing illustrations of the animals, sea life, climate, geography, and/or people of an island setting such as Karana's island. You may cut pictures from magazines, newspapers, old books, or any other available source. Arrange them attractively on a large piece of posterboard.

Publishing a Museum Guide

At the Southwest Museum in Los Angeles, artifacts from San Nicolas Island (Karana's island) may be seen. Imagine you are the curator of this museum and you wish to publish a booklet informing visitors about what they can see in the various exhibits in the museum. Write a museum guide with descriptions and illustrations of items found in excavations of Karana's island. Publish this in booklet form with a cover, title page, author, publisher, and copyright date. Be sure your descriptions and illustrations are both accurate and attractive.

Designing Your Own Project

If you can think of another project that will clearly demonstrate your knowledge of the text, you may substitute it for one of the projects listed above. Talk with your teacher about this.

SARAH, PLAIN AND TALL
Patricia MacLachlan
Harper & Row, 1985

PRAIRIE SONGS
Pam Conrad
Harper & Row, 1985

These two books tell of the courageous people who settled the prairies and of the deep emotional ties these people felt for their land. Sarah, a mail-order bride, leaves her beloved Maine seacoast to meet her husband, son, and daughter, who are hoping for a wife and mother who sings. In *Prairie Songs*, the author describes the tragedy and heroism that were a part of everyday prairie life.

Vocabulary for *Sarah, Plain and Tall*

hearthstones (page 3)
windbreak (page 18)
mica (page 29)
primly (page 39)

pesky (page 12)
flax (page 21)
sand dune (page 29)
pungent (page 47)

bedding (page 14)
ragwort (page 24)
killdeer (page 37)

Vocabulary for *Prairie Songs*

paddy (page 2)
soddy (page 13)
taut (page 36)
skeptical (page 57)
linden (page 76)

refined (page 4)
frivolous (page 20)
stimulate (page 40)
scheme (page 58)
beau (page 77)

gunnysacks (page 7)
rousing (page 31)
muslin (page 42)
coddled (page 76)
hoisted (page 78)

From *Literature Circles*, 1992. Teacher Ideas Press • P.O. Box 6633 • Englewood, CO 80155-6633.

Tracing the Train Routes

Both of these books take place on the prairies of the United States. Only in *Prairie Songs*, however, is the location specifically mentioned—Grand Island, Nebraska. The families in the books had begun their journeys in different places: Sarah came from the coast of Maine; Sarah's friend, Maggie, came from Tennessee; and Emmeline came from New York City. In the 1850s, when settlement of the prairies was just gaining momentum, newcomers often arrived by train. Assume that this was true for Sarah, Maggie, and Emmeline, and go to the library and consult an atlas. Locate the coast of Maine, Tennessee, New York City, and Grand Island, Nebraska, on a map. Either draw or construct a map that shows these places of departure and trace the best route a train (or trains) would have taken to bring its passengers to the prairie around Grand Island, Nebraska. Give your map a railroad flavor by using railroad symbols and trains. To do this you may need to find information and pictures about early railroads.

Designing a Quilt

During the long prairie winters, pioneer families would spend hours making household necessities by hand. Quilting was one of these crafts. Scraps of used clothing and other cloth material were never wasted. The scraps were recycled into quilts that in turn provided warmth and decoration. A multitude of designs and patterns were used. Design a quilt like one that Sarah or Clara Downing might have made with the help of their children. You may use paints, colored paper, or fabric for this quilt; you may also decide on the size of the quilt. There are many books on quilting. One book that has excellent pictures and instructions is:

Nelson, Cyril I., and Carter Houck. *Treasury of American Quilts*. New York: Greenwich House, 1982.

Be prepared to hang up your quilt for public display.

Building a Soddy

On page 17 of *Prairie Songs* is a short description of how a sod house is built. Using this information and information you can find in the library, construct a miniature but authentic soddy made of "prairie brick." Place your soddy on a platform that allows you to include the yard and surrounding prairie described in the book.

Writing a Book of Similes

In both books the authors use similes to enhance the pictures they create with words. A simile usually begins with either the word *like* or the word *as*. It effectively communicates an idea by comparing one thing to another. For example, in *Prairie Songs* it says, "his very words spun away ... like a dry tumbleweed" (p. 42). On page 49 in the same book it says, "She looked like a walnut again." Similes help readers create mental pictures. In *Sarah, Plain and Tall*, it says on page 8 that "She snored in a high whistle ... like a teakettle." On page 20 it says, "the land rolls a little like the sea."

Find at least 10 examples of similes in the two books and make a book of similes. Place one simile on each page (don't forget to enclose the simile in quotation marks) and illustrate it. You may want to experiment with different art forms to do this. Try to capture the author's meaning in your illustrations. Put your book together with a cover, title page complete with publisher's information, endpapers, and text. This book can be cataloged and placed in the library after presentation day.

Comparing Two Environments

In both of these books, the characters often mention the contrast between the prairie and the eastern part of the United States. The most remarkable contrast is that between the prairie and the Maine seacoast as described in *Sarah,*

Plain and Tall. Often the authors use colors to emphasize similarities and differences. Go to the library and find pictures and information about the prairie and the seacoast of Maine. To help you visualize the Maine seacoast, you may want to look at the following picture book:

Olson, Arielle North. *The Lighthouse Keeper's Daughter.* Boston: Little, Brown, 1987.

Using watercolors, a watercolor-wash, or another medium of your choice, select scenes from the books and create pictures that represent what you have learned about the two different environments. Try to use colors that accurately depict the feelings the authors try to communicate through their use of color words. Include a variety of scenes (at least three) from each environment. To compare the two and to display your artwork, create a bulletin board that compares the prairie to the Maine seacoast. Use text to accompany your visuals.

Composing a Collage of Poetry

The characters in the two books were, at different times, heroic, funny, and tragic. The authors created strong feelings about each character with words. In *Prairie Songs* poetry is a favorite way to express feelings, and in *Sarah, Plain and Tall* poetry in the form of song is important. Compose a poetic writing or a song about at least five of the characters from the two books. When you are writing, remember that poetry doesn't always have to rhyme. Display your poetry in the form of a collage on a large piece of posterboard. Give each separate poem or song its own background. Choose a color that best symbolizes the emotion your piece conveys.

Designing Your Own Project

If you can think of a project that will clearly demonstrate your knowledge of these two texts, you may substitute it for one of the projects mentioned above. Talk with your teacher about this.

If you liked these books, you might also enjoy:

Turner, Ann. *Third Girl from the Left.* New York: Macmillan, 1986.

THE SIGN OF THE BEAVER

Elizabeth George Speare
Dell Publications, 1983

K. SERVATT

Twelve-year-old Matt is left on his own to protect the family cabin in the Maine wilderness. He is rescued from an attack of swarming bees by an Indian chief and his grandson, Attean. The boys come to know each other, and Matt is accepted by the tribe. Matt eventually has to choose between going with Attean's people and waiting for the uncertain return of his father.

Vocabulary

touchhole (page 5)
deacon (page 12)
incomprehensible (page 31)
contemptuous (page 41)
ramshackle (page 85)
breeches (page 102)
typhus (page 131)

johnnycake (page 5)
banked (page 16)
heathen (page 32)
mangy (page 52)
mortar (page 85)
manitou (page 107)

chinking (page 7)
burly (page 18)
nonchalantly (page 41)
pungent (page 78)
breechcloth (page 102)
puckery (page 121)

From *Literature Circles*, 1992. Teacher Ideas Press • P.O. Box 6633 • Englewood, CO 80155-6633.

Taping a Picture Book

During the time that *The Sign of the Beaver* took place, extended families were the norm. Grandparents usually lived with their children and their grandchildren. Read some picture books that talk about extended families and the important parts older people played in the younger people's lives. You might want to read the following books.

Bunting, Eve. *The Wednesday Surprise.* New York: Clarion Books, 1989.

dePaola, Tomie. *Now One Foot, Now the Other.* New York: G. P. Putnam's Sons, 1981.

MacLachlan, Patricia. *Through Grandpa's Eyes.* New York: Harper & Row, 1980.

Read three or four picture books that tell of the older person's role in the life of a younger family member. Make a chart that shows the relative and his/her contribution to the young person's life. Also, choose the picture book that your group likes best and make a tape of it that younger children can listen to as they follow along in the book. You'll need to have background music, appropriate sound effects, a sound that indicates when to turn the page, and different voices for the narrator and various characters. Be sure to have "wait" time between pages so children have ample time to look at the illustrations. You'll need to practice a lot before you do the actual taping. You may want to donate your tape to one of the lower elementary classrooms after your presentation.

Creating Your Own Family Tree

Each member of the group should do this project individually. Create a family tree showing relationships in your own family. Design a format for your family tree. Go back at least to your grandparents, but try to go back further than that. It would be nice if you had actual photographs to accompany your family tree.

Constructing Three-Sided Models

Two types of dwellings are mentioned in the book—a log house and an Indian lodge. Using the information in the book, construct a three-sided model of each dwelling. Show the inside as well as the outside of the structures. Be sure to include the furnishings, and make them as authentic as possible. You will probably need to consult books in the library to make your models historically accurate. Display the models in an attractive and geographically realistic setting.

Preparing a Meal

Prepare a meal "from scratch" that would have been appropriate for the time and setting of the book. You may need to make some ingredient substitutions, but try to make the meal as authentic as possible. Fix enough food so the entire class will be able to taste each dish on presentation day. You may need to try out some of the recipes before presentation day (your family could be your "guinea pigs"). Make a recipe book that details the ingredients and preparation method for the dishes you cook. Look at recipe books in the library or at home to find the correct publication format for this type of book.

Designing Your Own Project

If you can think of another project that will clearly demonstrate your knowledge of the text, you may substitute it for one of the projects mentioned above. Talk with your teacher about this.

BLACK STAR, BRIGHT DAWN

Scott O'Dell
Fawcett Juniper, 1988

Bright Dawn's father asked her to take his place in the 1,000-mile-long Iditarod race between Anchorage and Nome. Together with Black Star, a wolf-husky cross, and the rest of her dog team, she begins the race. The story sensitively portrays Eskimo culture as the race winds its way across Alaska.

Vocabulary

leads (page 1)
floe (page 8)
mukluks (page 32)

caribou (page 3)
phobia (page 16)
derelict (page 74)

eewoonucks (page 6)
perilous (page 21)

From *Literature Circles*, 1992. Teacher Ideas Press • P.O. Box 6633 • Englewood, CO 80155-6633.

Mapping the Race

Bright Dawn is an Eskimo girl who lives, in the first part of the story, in an Eskimo village called Womengo. Consult an atlas to find the location of Womengo. Draw a map that pinpoints its location. The family moves to Ikuma. Locate Ikuma also and place it on your map. Add to your map the route of the race as the book progresses. Be sure to consult the atlas as you add each new point on the map.

Charting Customs and Beliefs

Eskimos have many customs and beliefs that seem strange to us (tying a leather rope across the room under the ceiling, for example). Find other examples of Eskimo customs or beliefs in the text. Think of American customs, beliefs, and even superstitions, and list them. Make a chart that explains Eskimo beliefs and American beliefs. You may need to do some research in the library to adequately complete this project.

Building a Dog Sled

What does a dog sled look like? Find a picture of the type of dog sled used in the one-thousand-plus-mile-long Iditarod. Using whatever medium you feel would be best, create a replica of the sled. Use information found in the text to help you build the sled.

Making a "How to" Book

Because you are a seasoned Iditarod racer, you have been asked by a publisher to write a book that tells new or first-time racers how to race the Iditarod. Look at other "how to" books in the library. Following their format, create your own book entitled "How to Race the Iditarod." Include illustrations to enhance your instructions.

Advertising the Iditarod

You are an advertising agent for the Iditarod. You must create an entire campaign. Make use of all media, including posters, handbills, radio ads (on a tape recorder—be sure you have background music), TV ads (use a video camera if you can), newspaper ads (black and white), and magazine ads (color). Think carefully about the components of a good ad. Look at ads on billboards, in newspapers, and in magazines. What do the ads have in common? Listen to ads on the radio. Listen to and look at ads on television. Be creative, and entice people to enter the race.

Choosing an Illustrator

The author creates vivid word pictures in readers' minds, but there are no illustrations in the book. Choose eight scenes from the book and find illustrations in picture books that would fit with your choice of scenes. Write down the scenes and the corresponding illustrations. You may use several different picture books to complete this project. Be sure to write down the title, author, and page number of each picture book so you will know exactly where to find the illustrations when you do your presentation to the class. Do you think one illustrator would be better suited for *Black Star, Bright Dawn*? Why?

Drawing a Legend

The legend of Raven begins at the end of chapter 8. Using only pictures, draw the legend. Incorporate all the things Mr. Oteg says about Raven. When you present this to the class, you may use words to enhance your visual representation of the legend.

Designing Your Own Project

If you can think of another project that will clearly demonstrate your knowledge of the text, you may substitute it for one of the projects mentioned above. Talk with your teacher about this.

HATCHET
Gary Paulsen
Puffin Books, 1987

Brian is flying to Canada to visit his father for the summer when the pilot suddenly has a heart attack, and the small plane crashes into a remote lake. Brian's only survival tool is a parting gift from his mother: a hatchet. He comes to terms with his life situation and survives in the wilderness for over 50 days.

Vocabulary

clawed (page 2)
jolts (page 11)
diminish (page 57)
slithering (page 80)
dung (page 143)

slewed (page 4)
massively (page 35)
pulverized (page 58)
convulse (page 101)
stymied (page 168)

spasm (page 10)
relative (page 46)
wuffling (page 74)
corrosive (page 130)
furor (page 194)

Finding the Lake

Brian left the small airport in Hampton, New York, and headed toward the oil fields of Canada, "up on the tree line where the tundra started and the forests ended." Look in the library in an atlas to see where this place might be located. Chapters 1 and 2 describe the flight. Figure out how long Brian was in the air, how fast a plane (Cessna 406) travels, and how far from Hampton Brian might have gone. Use the topographical clues given in the text and decide where in Canada you think Brian's lake was. Draw a map of this area and chart Brian's probable course of flight.

Learning from Mistakes

Chapter 14 talks about the many mistakes Brian made and how he learned from these mistakes. Make a chart that lists these mistakes and any other mistakes you think Brian made. Opposite of the mistake listing, note what Brian learned from that particular mistake. We have all made mistakes, many of them, in our lifetimes. Hopefully, we learned from them as Brian did. Make a list of your mistakes and what they taught you. You may present this information in the form of a chart, a poem, a play, a pantomime, or any other form you think would be appropriate.

Constructing a Shelter

During his stay at the lake, Brian built and lived in two very different shelters. Find descriptions of both of these shelters in the text. Using the information you find, construct both shelters from materials like the ones Paulsen describes. In your presentation you will need to point out the features in the second shelter that made it better than the first.

Keeping a Secret

Brian often thinks and dreams about the Secret. At the end of the story, he considers telling his father about it. Why doesn't he? Why is it better not to tell some things? Create a questionnaire for your fellow classmates about secrets. What makes them "keep" rather than "tell" some things? Do they have secrets of their own that they don't divulge to anyone? What kinds of things do they tell to one or two close friends? What kinds of things do they keep to themselves? Be sure to word the questionnaire so no one actually tells either a secret of their own or anyone else's. Make some kind of chart that shows the results of your questionnaire.

Creating a Field Guide

Brian lived alone in the Canadian wilderness for 54 days. During that time he learned much about the plants and animals that shared his environment. Imagine you are Brian. You have been asked by the Canadian Wilderness Association to create a guide to the plants and animals of the area. The guide should list the plants and animals (include fish), give a short description of each, and have accompanying illustrations. Put your information in the form of a field guide. Use a published field guide as a source for your own publication. The information in the epilogue will be helpful to you as you decide what plants and animals to include.

Making Survival Tools

Survival was of the utmost importance to Brian. To survive, he had to make many tools and utensils. Find a description of one of these items in the text. Using materials you find outside, fashion a tool or utensil of your own that is somewhat similar to something Brian made in the story. Show your item to the class on presentation day, describe how you made it, and tell how it would be used.

Designing Your Own Project

If you can think of a project that will clearly demonstrate your knowledge of the book, you may substitute it for one of the above projects. Talk with your teacher about this.

THE INDIAN IN THE CUPBOARD
Lynne Reid Banks
Avon Books, 1982

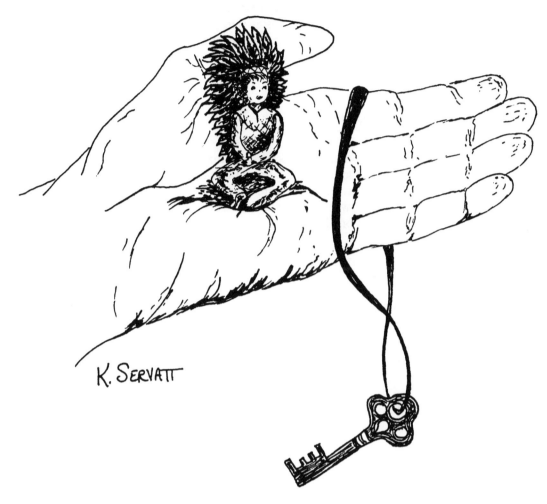

K. SERVATT

Miniature figures come to life when the key is turned in the cupboard in which they are kept. Omri learns responsibility as he awakens his cache of little people with a turn of a key. A spirit of imagination and fantasy prevail even as serious subjects are explored.

Vocabulary

compost (page 1)
plait (page 11)
appalled (page 15)
escarpment (page 39)
"three sisters" (pages 51 and 62)
firelighters (page 71)
myriad (page 144)

coherent (page 7)
intricate (page 11)
"firewater" (page 18)
quiverful (page 52)
maize (page 62)
mulish (page 76)
joists (page 158)

ferociously (page 10)
tantalizing (page 13)
ransacked (page 30)
ungrateful (page 57)
marrow (page 62)
bafflement (page 134)

From *Literature Circles*, 1992. Teacher Ideas Press • P.O. Box 6633 • Englewood, CO 80155-6633.

Finding Similarities and Differences

Little Bear was an Iroquois who spoke often of his enemies, the Algonquin. Go to the library and find information about these two northeastern Native American groups. You may also refer to page 51 in the text. Find likenesses and differences in their food, transportation, homes and shelters, clothing, customs, religious beliefs, and art symbols (p. 27). Organize and arrange your information on a poster-size piece of paper in chart form. On this chart use symbols to represent the main topics listed above and list your information under Iroquois and Algonquin. Make a key that defines the symbols to accompany your chart. You may use drawn or cut-out pictures as well as written text to communicate your information.

Examining the French and Indian War

Little Bear referred to the French and Indian War. Some information about this war is given on pages 29 and 54 of the text. Go to the library and find additional information about this American war during the 1700s. Who was fighting? Who were allies, and who were enemies? Why were they at war? Where was this war fought? Take notes on your findings. Make and label a map that shows the important battles and areas involved in the war. Include the territories of the Iroquois and Algonquin tribes on this map.

Constructing a Cupboard

Construct a cupboard with small compartments that contain items representative of the book. The author provides colorful descriptions of characters and inanimate objects. Referring to these will help you authentically reproduce the miniatures. For example, Tommy Adkins on page 43, the horse on page 33, the old chief on page 58, and Boone's sketch on page 131 are vividly described. You may choose to make your cupboard either two- or three-dimensional.

Building Indian Dwellings

The Iroquois lived in longhouses (p. 55), and the Algonquin lived in tepees (p. 26). Using authentic materials as often as possible, construct a longhouse and a tepee. To each shelter attach a label telling why the particular tribe used certain materials, how each home was typically constructed, and why each shelter suited the lifestyle of the group. Also describe the family structure that was involved in the use of the shelter.

Writing a Comic Book

Look at examples of Classic Comic Books. These are available at newsstands and bookstores. Choose one chapter of *The Indian in the Cupboard* that has picturesque language and entertaining dialogue. Using the characters and actual quotations as they appear in the book, rewrite this chapter in the style and format of a Classic Comic Book. Be careful to keep the meaning of the language as the author uses it.

Surveying the Class

Lynne Reid Banks has said that she did not enjoy reading when she was young because she didn't like the kinds of children's books that were available at the time. She wrote *The Indian in the Cupboard* and its sequels thinking that kids would enjoy them. If you were an author of young adult books, what kinds of books would you write? Survey your class and at least one other class to find out what topics interest students your age. Make a double bar graph to demonstrate the results of this survey. You may color-code the classes to show the results more clearly. Go to the library to get biographical data on Banks. Calculate the year in which she would have been your age. Look at card catalogs to find some young adult books that were published in or before this year. Compose a list of titles you think you might have enjoyed had you been growing up with Banks.

Designing Your Own Project

If you can think of another project that will clearly demonstrate your knowledge of the text, you may substitute it for one of the projects mentioned above. Talk with your teacher about this.

THE CAY
Theodore Taylor
Avon Books, 1969

Racial prejudice is examined in this book that is dedicated to Dr. Martin Luther King, Jr. A young white boy, blinded by an explosion on a ship, learns how to survive on an uninhabited island through the patient teaching of his only companion, an aged black man. Phillip learns that "black" is a color people see with their eyes rather than with their hearts.

Vocabulary

pontoon bridge (page 10)
afterholds (page 30)
scorch (page 45)
lurched (page 59)
rancid (page 80)
debris (page 120)

schooners (page 11)
haunches (page 31)
port (page 50)
palm fronds (page 67)
welted (page 104)
precise (page 123)

disheartened (page 24)
alabaster (page 32)
harassment (page 56)
catchment (page 77)
groped (page 119)

From *Literature Circles*, 1992. Teacher Ideas Press • P.O. Box 6633 • Englewood, CO 80155-6633.

Mapping the Location

The story begins in the port town of Willemstad on the island of Curacao off the coast of Venezuela. In an atlas in the library, find that island. Chapters 1 and 2 talk about this location and about the route the *Hato* was taking to get back to the United States. Draw a map of the area and trace the route the *Hato* had taken before it was torpedoed on April 6, 1942. Now, using other information you find in the text, trace the route you think Phillip and Timothy took in the raft to get to their island. When you show this map to the class during your presentation, be able to explain why you think the island is located where it is.

Reconstructing the Island

Chapters 11 and 13 describe the island, its shape, basic topography, and the outlying reefs. Reconstruct the island from clay, salt dough, or any other medium with which you feel comfortable. When you have finished the island and surrounding areas, add the "man-made" items.

Listing Survival Methods

Timothy did several things after the arrival on the island to assure Phillip's survival. Carefully look through the text and find the things Timothy did. List them. After you have listed them, tell why each thing was so important for Phillip's survival. You may want to put this information on a chart to use as a visual aid in your presentation.

Investigating Prejudice

The author's description of Timothy begins on page 31. Reread this description. What specific words and phrases does the author use to tell you how Phillip feels about the black man? This story of overcoming prejudice occurs during World War II. Read *Nettie's Trip South*, a story that describes prejudice in the pre-Civil War time in the United States.

Turner, Ann. *Nettie's Trip South*. New York: Macmillan, 1987.

This book is based on a true story. What specific words and phrases does Turner use to describe white people's feelings toward blacks? List the similarities found in both texts. Phillip's feelings toward Timothy change as the story progresses. Nettie's feelings toward the injustice accorded the slaves she sees intensify.

The Cay is dedicated to Dr. Martin Luther King, Jr. Who was he? Why would Taylor dedicate this particular book to Dr. King? Prepare a dialogue between Phillip, Nettie, and Dr. Martin Luther King, Jr. Think carefully about their feelings about racial prejudice. You may choose to present this dialogue in any form you wish. Be sure to give the class background information on each of the three participants in the dialogue. You may want to read aloud *Nettie's Trip South*. You may want to choose a "live" or videotaped interview with the participants, an "I Am the Character" presentation, a question-and-answer session in which selected class members have been given predetermined questions to ask, or a "talk show" format. Choose the method that best suits your group. Whatever method you choose, be well informed and well prepared.

Creating a Monument

Imagine Phillip is now an adult. He does find and return to the island on which he and Timothy lived. He decides to create a permanent monument to Timothy at his gravesite. What will this monument look like? What will Phillip do so that anyone who sees it will know the "greatness" of Timothy? You may actually build this monument, or you may draw a picture of it.

Being Blind

Be blind for a day at school. Choose one of the other group members to be your "eyes" as Timothy was Phillip's "eyes." Each member of the group should do this experiment. Be sure to explain to all of your teachers what you are doing and the reason for it. At the conclusion of your day, write a poem that expresses your feelings about blindness. Put these poems together in a book. Use the correct form for a book. To whom will your group dedicate the book?

Designing Your Own Project

If you can think of another project that will clearly demonstrate your knowledge of the book, you may substitute it for one of the projects mentioned above. Talk with your teacher about this.

THE INCREDIBLE JOURNEY
Sheila Burnford
Bantam Skylark, 1960

K. SERVATT

Three domestic animals, a cat and two dogs, make an incredible journey across the Canadian wilderness to return to their home and their owners. The story of the three animals' adventures as they conquer the wild and the people they meet along the way is courageous, witty, and heartfelt.

Vocabulary

amphibious (page 2)
contrition (page 6)
incessant (page 13)
ineffectual (page 36)
galvanizing (page 38)
forage (page 41)
mirth (page 47)
clamorous (page 54)
debris (page 65)
zealous (page 77)
capitulated (page 81)
poseur (page 94)
raucous (page 100)
infinitesimal (page 113)
savor (page 141)

panorama (page 2)
sybaritic (page 7)
placid (page 20)
adversary (page 36)
harlequin (page 38)
ingratiatingly (page 45)
succored (page 49)
marauding (page 55)
requiem (page 66)
sinuous (page 78)
insolence (page 86)
wanton (page 95)
porcine (page 106)
replete (page 122)

docile (page 4)
thrall (page 10)
retched (page 29)
bravado (page 37)
succulent (page 39)
paroxysms (page 46)
nomadic (page 53)
irresolute (page 59)
heraldic (page 74)
wraith (page 79)
pliant (page 88)
malevolent (page 97)
gargoyle (page 109)
conjured (page 138)

From *Literature Circles*, 1992. Teacher Ideas Press • P.O. Box 6633 • Englewood, CO 80155-6633.

Tracing the Route

Many clues are given in the text as to the route the three animals took to reach their destination. Go through the book and list the places mentioned in the order that they appear. Go to the library and, using an atlas, find a map of Canada. Try to locate some or all of the places mentioned in the book. Draw a map of Canada and trace the route that the two dogs and the cat followed as they made the long journey home to their respective masters.

Drawing the Encounters

During the long journey, the cat and the two dogs encountered many people and animals—some friendly, some not. Create a pictorial representation of these encounters. You may draw the meetings or use cut-out pictures. Write a one-sentence synopsis of each encounter. You may choose to put these together as a bound book, a "big" book, a mural, or a "trip encounter map." Be creative and imaginative.

Researching Siamese Cats

Helvi Nurmi, after finding the almost drowned Siamese cat and taking him to her home, got two books from the traveling library about Siamese cats. The description about what she found begins on page 76 of the text. Go to the library and find out as much as you can about this breed of cat. Put your information together and present it in the form of a TV documentary. You will need visuals to accompany your verbal text (a live Siamese cat would be great). You may choose to videotape your presentation and play it back for the class, or you may choose to present "live" TV. Be sure to practice before the taping or the "live" broadcast.

Making a Field Guide

Many species of wild animals are mentioned in *The Incredible Journey*. Make an alphabetized field guide that pictures all of the animals mentioned in the story. Give a brief description of each animal. Put your information together in the form of a bound book. Be sure to use a standard format for the book. Use a field guide from the library as an example to follow.

Writing Poems

The book begins with an excerpt from Walt Whitman's *Leaves of Grass* entitled "The Beasts." Write, in poetry form, an ending to the book. Become each of the three animals and, writing in the first person, describe your journey and how you felt as you were travelling the hundreds of miles to your final destination. You may write three separate poems, write one narrative poem that includes the three characters, or write a poem for three voices. If you choose to write a poem for three voices, use the following books by Paul Fleischman as references.

Fleischman, Paul. *I Am Phoenix.* New York: Harper & Row, 1985.

_____. *Joyful Noise.* New York: Trumpet Club, 1988.

Designing Your Own Project

If you can think of another project that will clearly demonstrate your knowledge of the text, you may substitute it for one of the projects mentioned above. Talk with your teacher about this.

THE WESTING GAME
Ellen Raskin
Avon Books, 1978

Establishing all 16 players in an apartment in the glistening Sunset Towers apartment building on the shore of Lake Michigan, Samuel W. Westing deals out clues to the solution of a puzzle that could reward any of the participants with his $200 million legacy. He has made only one mistake. Only the reader has all the clues to the puzzle.

Vocabulary

spasms (page 9)
putrid (page 15)
simpered (page 25)
bigot (page 44)
paraphernalia (page 70)
docket (page 115)

pivoted (page 9)
pyrotechnic (page 19)
elfin (page 33)
vindictiveness (page 48)
harried (page 73)
appellate (page 127)

facade (page 11)
trousseau (page 23)
inscrutable (page 44)
chiding (page 59)
obsequious (page 83)
paranoia (page 150)

From *Literature Circles*, 1992. Teacher Ideas Press • P.O. Box 6633 • Englewood, CO 80155-6633.

Mapping the Location

Sunset Towers (which faced east) was on the shore of Lake Michigan. Look in an atlas for Lake Michigan. Draw a map of the lake and place Sunset Towers in the appropriate place. Be sure the apartment building is drawn according to the description in the text.

Describing the Characters

Do a character description of each of the 16 players in "the Westing game" (Madame Sun Lin Hoo, Turtle Wexler, Christos Theodorakis, Jake Wexler, Flora Baumbach, D. Denton Deere, Alexander McSouthers, J. J. Ford, Grace Windsor Wexler, James Shin Hoo, Berthe Erica Crow, Otis Amber, Theo Theodorakis, Doug Hoo, Sydelle Pulaski, and Angela Wexler). Be sure to include the information given in chapters 28 and 29. Create a character chart to show how the characters are related to one another.

Writing a Will

Samuel W. Westing's will is written in chapters 6 and 7. In the library, find out what is usually included in a last will and testament. Westing's will is not typical. Choose a character from a book you have all read, and, following the correct form, write a will for that character. (If you cannot find a character in common, choose a character from a picure book that you can read together.)

Making a Board Game

Could you create a mystery board game? You might want to look at the game *Clue* and take some hints and strategies from it. You'll need to make the board, the playing pieces, and the directions. Play the game in your group to make sure it works.

Creating an Audiocassette

There are many mystery picture books. The Piggins series by Jane Yolen and the Miss Nelson series by Harry Allard are quite good. Read a few of these picture books and find one your group particularly enjoys. Your job is to create an audiocassette for beginning readers or nonreaders that accompanies the text. You'll need to give instructions to the listeners/readers at the beginning of the tape, have a sound that indicates when to turn the page, provide "wait" time to allow readers to look at the illustrations, include background music (either create your own or use appropriate prerecorded music), and record the text itself. Practice a lot before you record your story.

Designing Your Own Project

If you can think of another project that will clearly demonstrate your knowledge of the text, you may substitute it for one of the projects mentioned above. Talk with your teacher about this.

WHERE THE RED FERN GROWS
Wilson Rawls
Bantam Starfire, 1983

K. SERVATT

Old Dan and Little Ann are 10-year-old Billy's "dream come true" and the prize coon dogs of the northeastern Oklahoma hill country. This story gives special meaning to the Native American legend of the red fern. A boy and his dogs win and lose in the game of life as they travel within the story through which the legend unfolds.

Vocabulary

quench (page 5)
domain (page 77)
begrudgingly (page 125)
dumbfounded (page 156)
berserk (page 225)

haunches (page 19)
squalls (page 96)
brute (page 144)
canebrakes (page 201)

bored (page 40)
flinty (page 114)
protruding (page 146)
mantel (page 220)

From *Literature Circles*, 1992. Teacher Ideas Press • P.O. Box 6633 • Englewood, CO 80155-6633.

Planting a Terrarium

The Ozarks described in the book are located in eastern Oklahoma. However, the Ozarks as a region extend into Missouri and Arkansas. Go to the library and find out about the geography of the Ozarks. What is the vegetation like? What kinds of plants and trees grow in the Ozarks? Make a chart that compares the flora and fauna of the Ozark region to the flora and fauna of the region of the country in which you live. Be able to tell why the vegetation is alike or different. Plant either one divided or two separate terrariums showing the two kinds of vegetation. The library will have books that tell how to plant a terrarium.

Making a Moonlight Shadow Box

Many "night" scenes are depicted in the novel. Choose one of them and make a shadow box that illustrates the scene. Imagine that the hold in the top of the box that lets in light is moonlight illuminating your chosen scene. You may have to rearrange the scenery in the box to make the best use of your "moonlight."

Choosing the Dog for You

If you could have any kind of dog you wanted, what breed would you choose? Research this breed. List the attributes and tell why it would be a good dog for you. Find sources for obtaining such a dog. Choose one of the sources and write a letter of inquiry. What questions will you ask the seller?

Creating a Survey

Most people have a favorite kind of pet. Create a survey about favorite pets to give to classmates, friends, and family. After the survey has been completed, use a single or double bar graph or a circle graph to chart the results.

Writing a Legend

The legend of the red fern is found on page 246. It is a Native American legend of "life after death." Many legends and myths were created so people could understand natural phenomena for which they had no scientific knowledge. What are some well-known myths and legends that explain natural phenomena? You may want to look specifically at Greek myths and Native American legends. Write your own "life after death" legend.

Making Tombstones

Even though Billy did not like Rubin, he felt very badly about Rubin's accidental death. Keeping in mind Billy's feelings about Rubin as a person, write an epitaph that Billy might have written to put on Rubin's tombstone. Make a tombstone and write the epitaph on it. If Rainie had not become "ill" after his brother's death, what would he have written on Rubin's tombstone? Also, make tombstones for Dan and Ann. What would Billy have written on them? Think about how Grandpa felt about Billy and his dogs. What would Grandpa have written on the dogs' tombstones?

Designing Your Own Project

If you can think of another project that will clearly demonstrate your knowledge of the text, you may substitute it for one of the projects mentioned above. Talk with your teacher about this.

THE BONE WARS
Kathryn Lasky
Puffin Books, 1988

During General George Custer's pursuit of the Sioux and the Cheyenne in the 1800s, two young boys, both members of paleontology expeditions, meet, going on to discover relics of their own. Much of the story is factual, and it is based on expeditions logged by two renowned paleontologists of the time.

Vocabulary

raked (page 5)
notorious (page 9)
affront (page 20)
hansom (page 39)
depredatious (page 89)
vehemence (page 150)
ossified (page 202)

protruding (page 5)
fossilized (page 12)
pungent (page 27)
intrepid (page 63)
escarpment (page 118)
garrulousness (page 153)
callow (page 220)

acuity (page 9)
precedence (page 17)
magnate (page 37)
chafing (page 69)
defile (page 127)
goaded (page 165)

From *Literature Circles*, 1992. Teacher Ideas Press • P.O. Box 6633 • Englewood, CO 80155-6633.

Discovering the Pterosaur

Read the author's notes that begin on page 371. The paleontologists in the story are based on real people who "dug" in the area described in the book in the 1870s and 1880s. O. C. Marsh actually discovered the fossilized remains of one of the first pterosaurs. What is a pterosaur? Make a poster that shows the pterosaur, tells its size, and describes its habitat. Be sure to tell why it is *not* a dinosaur. The following book might help you find this information.

Norman, David, and Angela Milner. *Dinosaur.* New York: Alfred A. Knopf, 1989.

Portraying the Characters

Many of the characters in the book are given their real names: Sitting Bull, Crazy Horse, Black Elk, General George Custer, Buffalo Bill Cody, and Calamity Jane. Each member in your group should portray one of these characters. Create a dialogue in which the characters talk about how they were depicted in the story. You may choose to write and present this in any way that you find interesting and compatible to the subject. You may need to find additional information on the characters to present this project.

Making a Tipi

On page 49 the author describes the pictures on the tipi of Black Elk. Using these descriptions as your basis, reconstruct the tipi complete with pictures. If Thad lived in a tipi, what pictures would be painted on it? Make Thad's tipi also.

Writing a Poem for Two Voices

If you are not familiar with poems for two voices, look at two books by Paul Fleischman.

Fleischman, Paul. *I Am Phoenix.* New York: Harper & Row, 1985.

_____. *Joyful Noise.* New York: Trumpet Club, 1988.

Thad and Julian are two very different people who have very similar interests. Write a poem for two voices in which Thad is one of the voices and Julian is the other. Be sure to use the format created by Paul Fleischman. After you have written the poem, practice it in preparation for presenting it to the class.

Creating a Predictable Picture Book

Predictable books are written for young, beginning readers. They have a pattern and/or a rhyme with which readers can identify. Your librarian can help you find examples of predictable books to peruse. Write a predictable picture book about paleontology. The science of paleontology is described very simply in the following books.

Baylor, Byrd. *If You Are a Hunter of Fossils.* New York: Macmillan, 1980.

Brandenberg, Aliki. *Digging Up Dinosaurs.* New York: Thomas A. Crowell, 1981.

Be prepared to read your book to the entire class.

Investigating the Battle of the Little Bighorn

Pages 279 and 280 in the text describe the beginnings of the hostilities between the Sioux and the Cheyenne and the Bluecoats. The remainder of the book talks about the various battles that preceded Little Bighorn and the battle of

Little Bighorn itself. Using a historical source, find out about this battle. Is Lasky's portrayal accurate? Make a chart that shows in what areas the author sticks to historical facts and in which areas she fictionalizes the encounter between the Native Americans and the U.S. soldiers.

Designing Your Own Project

If you can think of another project that will clearly demonstrate your knowledge of the text, you may substitute it for one of the projects mentioned above. Talk with your teacher about this.

Index

Abilene, Kansas, 54
Adler, David, 32
Afro-American dialect, 19
Aleutian Islands (Alaska), 71
Algonquin, 84
Allard, Harry, 35, 92
Alliteration, 41
The Amazing Apple Book, 65
Anaya, Rudolfo A., 48
Animals, 51, 77, 89-90, 93-94
   Arctic, 52
Appalachian folk art, 65-66
Appalachian Mountains, 64

Babbitt, Natalie, 42
The Ballad of Belle Dorcas, 48
Banks, Lynne Reid, 83
Battle of the Little Bighorn, 96-97
Baylor, Byrd, 96
Beatty, Patricia, 64
Before Going to the Library checklist, 8, 14
Bemelmans, Ludwig, 35
Birthday parties, 26
Black Elk, 96
Black Star, Bright Dawn, 77-79
Blindness, 86-88
Blue Ridge Mountains (Virginia), 65
Board games, 92
The Bone Wars, 95-97
Book covers, 48
Book talks, 1
Bourgeois, Paulette, 65
Brandenberg, Aliki, 96
Brett, Jan, 20, 51
Buffalo Bill, 96
Building projects, 18, 24, 45, 51, 63, 73, 76, 78, 81, 84,
    94, 96. *See also* Model rooms
Bunyan, Paul, 48
Burnford, Sheila, 89
Byars, Betsy, 23-24, 39-41

Calamity, Jane, 96
Canada, 80, 81, 89, 90
Canyon de Chelly, Arizona, 68
Cartoon strips, making, 35
Carving, 52
Castles, 62-63
Cats, 89-90
Cattle drives, 54
The Cay, 86-88
Characters
   historical, 96
   stereotypical, 22

Charley Skedaddle, 5, 64-66
Charts, 54, 92
Checklists. *See* Reproducible pages
China
   calendar, 32
   customs compared with U.S. customs, 32
Chisolm Trail, 54
Chronicles of Narnia, 34, 35
Civil War (U.S.), 64-65
Clifton, Lucille, 54
Coats-of-arms, designing, 63
Cody, Buffalo Bill, 96
Cohen, Barbara, 32
Cole, Joanna, 35
Collages, 24, 37, 71, 74
Comic books, writing, 84
Commander Toad series, 35
Comparing books by the same author, 19
Conrad, Pam, 72
Cooking, 37, 48, 76. *See also* Foods; Recipes
Cooperative learning, defined, xiii
Crazy Horse, 96
Cupboards, constructing, 84
Curacao, 87
Custer, General George, 96

Daily Checklist, 8, 11
de Angeli, Marguerite, 62
Denmark, 57
Dialect, 19
Differences, 60, 84
Digging Up Dinosaurs, 96
Dinosaur, 96
Dinosaurs, 96
Dog sleds, 78
Dogs, 77, 89-90, 93-94
The Door in the Wall, 62-63
Drawings. *See* Illustrators and illustrating

Enright, Elizabeth, 44
Eskimos, 50, 77-78
Eulogies, 65
Everett Anderson's Goodbye, 54

Families, bibliography, 76
Family trees, 76
Fancy eggs, 22
The Farolitos of Christmas, 48
Field guides, 81, 90
Finding Descriptors along the Way checklist, 8, 15
The First Dog, 51

About the Authors

Mimi Neamen

Mimi received her B.A. from the University of Texas at El Paso and her M.Ed. from the University of New Mexico. She is currently working on her educational specialist degree from the University of New Mexico. She recently published two articles, "Picture Books in the Middle School" in the *New Mexico English Journal* and "Literary Challenge: A Battle with Books" in *The New Mexico Journal of Reading*. In 1991 she and a colleague received a Quality Education Award for their development of "Literary Challenge: A Battle with Books." Mimi's interest in reading and literature and her involvement in the Rio Grande Writing Project have been the basis of many professional presentations.

Mimi teaches sixth grade language arts, literature, and creative writing and eighth grade enriched English at the Roosevelt Middle School in Tijeras, New Mexico, the smallest middle school in the Albuquerque Public School District. She lives with her husband and five children near Tijeras where she watches baseball and coaches and plays softball.

Mary Strong

Mary received her B.A. from the University of New Mexico and recently completed her M.Ed. through the Teacher Enhancement Program, a collaborative program for midcareer teachers between the University of New Mexico and the Albuquerque Public School District. Mary and Mimi have made numerous presentations on literature circles and cooperative learning.

Mary teaches fifth grade at A. Montoya Elementary School in Tijeras, New Mexico. She lives with her husband in Tijeras, where they are building a mountain home, now that their three children are grown and on their own.

www.ingramcontent.com/pod-product-compliance
Ingram Content Group UK Ltd.
Pitfield, Milton Keynes, MK11 3LW, UK
UKHW012331270225
455688UK00010B/283